ORIGINAL

MORRIS MINOR

ORIGINAL
MORRIS MINOR

RAY NEWELL

PHOTOGRAPHY BY JOHN COLLEY
EDITED BY MARK HUGHES

BAY VIEW
BOOKS

Published 1993 by Bay View Books Ltd
13a Bridgeland Street
Bideford, Devon EX39 2QE

© Copyright 1993 by Bay View Books Ltd
Designed by Peter Laws
Typesetting by Chris Fayers

ISBN 1 870979 43 5
Printed in Hong Kong

CONTENTS

INTRODUCTION

The single-piece windscreen and modified roof panel introduced for the new Morris Minor 1000 in 1956 are clear to see in this unusual overhead shot.

Having been closely involved with the Morris Minor scene for the past 12 years, both as an enthusiastic owner and as an official of the Morris Minor Owners' Club (MMOC), I am conscious of the continuing enthusiasm for this car in all its guises. I never cease to be amazed at the interest in the history of Morris Minors, particularly in the quest for information about their original specifications.

I had recognised the important contribution the *Original* series has been making in providing reference sources about originality for owners of other marques, so to be asked to write *Original Morris Minor* was an unexpected compliment. While delighted about this opportunity, I have to admit that it has proved to be a challenging and sometimes very demanding task which I could not have undertaken without the support, assistance and understanding of many people.

First and foremost is our photographer, John Colley, who drew the short straw in his first *Original* book. While the established formula of the series has been adhered to, the sheer number of cars that have had to be photographed in order to do justice to the model range has had to be greatly increased. The photographs, a vitally important part of

the book, speak volumes not only about the vehicles themselves and their original features, but they also say a great deal about the quality of John's work and the rapport he struck up with all the owners.

The owners who very generously allowed their vehicles to be photographed are as follows: Keith Fletcher (Series MM tourer and 1000 convertible), Barry Norman (Series MM two-door saloon), Bryan Gostling (Series II Traveller), Trevor Lammas (Series II convertible), Alan Prest (Series II saloon), Ian Millington (1000 four-door saloon), Barry Tibbetts (1000 two-door saloon), John Ford (1000 two-door saloon), Mike Taylor (1000 four-door saloon), Harry Cook (1000 Traveller), Martin O'Dowd (Series II pick-up), Brian Fletcher (Series II van), Neville Wright (1000 pick-up and Austin van), Ian Hawkes (Austin pick-up), Pete Hanby (Series II GPO engineers' van), Dave Preston (Morris GPO mail van), Colin Ellis (Morris GPO mail van) and Roland Turner (Morris GPO telephones van).

Thanks are due to all these owners for their patience and their efforts in preparing and presenting their vehicles, sometimes in far from ideal weather conditions. In addition, various MMOC members kindly made their vehicles available for photography at the

The 4in wide swage up the centre of all Morris Minor bonnets is a reminder of an eleventh hour decision to widen the prototype design for production. This bonnet badge was introduced for the Series II versions in 1952/53 and remained in use to the end of production in 1971.

Author Ray Newell's thorough coverage extends to all commercial versions, such as this 1969 Post Office mail van (below).

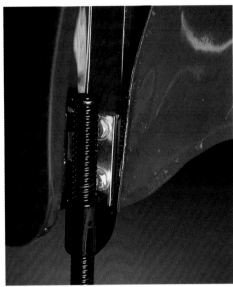

This shot of a Series MM screw jack in use at a front jacking point is typical of the close-up photographic detail featured throughout this book.

1992 Series MM Rally at Nuffield Place (the home of William Morris), the 1992 National Rally at Billing Aquadrome, and on location during photo sessions for the 1992/93 MMOC calendars.

Attempting to detail the changes which occurred during the 22-year production run of the Morris Minor is no mean feat. In tackling this daunting task, I have relied heavily on the wisdom of a small group of fellow enthusiasts who, like me, have a particular affinity for seeing the Minor in its original state. I'm grateful to them for putting up with my questioning. One of my lasting memories of this book is the task of rewriting various sections as a result of protracted debate resulting from their deliberations, research and experience. Heartfelt thanks go to Peter Gamble and Keith Fletcher (Series MM), Bryan Gostling and Ian Murray (Series II), Martin Flanders (Minor 1000, 948cc and 1098cc), Brian Fletcher and Neville Wright (Light

Commercials), and Peter Hanby (Series II Commercials and Post Office vehicles).

Special mention should also be made in this respect to Chris Spink of the Post Office Vehicle Club for very comprehensive information on these Minors, and to Rick Feibush and Tony Burgess of the Morris Minor Registry in America for arranging photographs and providing additional information on American models. Arnold Wilson also plugged a few gaps by supplying some Series II pictures, and detail shots relating to some of the special option vehicles were supplied by Paul Bailey, Robin Everall and Gerry Cambridge. I am also indebted to Martin Flanders for the effort made in sorting and transporting his treasure trove of original parts for the studio photography in the restoration chapter.

Original sources have been a vital component in putting together details of production, trim and paint specifications, and change points. In this respect I am

indebted to the British Motor Industry Heritage Trust for allowing me access to their records and to archivist – and fellow *Original* series author – Anders Clausager for providing additional information to what had already been researched by him and released for publication, particularly in relation to the introduction and discontinuation of paint colours.

Finally, a word of thanks to Sue Bonnington, who has worked with me in the preparation of the manuscript, and to my long-suffering family, who have been supportive in allowing me the time and space to get on with the job.

A note of explanation is necessary concerning my use of the terms tourer and convertible. Both are in common usage, but I have adopted a clear distinction: tourers are Series MM models with detachable sidescreens, whereas all later open cars with fixed window frames are described as convertibles. Some confusion has arisen because the designation 'tourer' remained part of the chassis identification code throughout production, even though contemporary sales literature generally described all but the earlier Series MM versions as convertibles.

If this book makes owners feel more confident about tackling the restoration of their Morris Minors, and if it assists them in returning their cars to something near original specification, then the task will have been worthwhile. If it is any consolation or inspiration, I've also learned a great deal while researching and writing the text.

Ray Newell
May 1993

MORRIS MINOR PAST & PRESENT

The appeal of the Morris Minor is so strong that for many people just the mention of the name evokes nostalgic memories. Images of the Minor extend far beyond the stereotype associations with vicars, district nurses, elderly ladies, postmen and travelling salesmen. Indeed, for many the memories are far more personal.

The Morris Minor was – and still is – regarded as part of the family, viewed as a friend, and even given pet names. Such affection for a mere car, while not unique to the Minor, is indicative of the esteem in which this true British classic is held. Enhanced by a reputation for reliability, durability and economy, it has remained a popular choice for everyday motoring and emerged as one of the most popular choices for classic car enthusiasts.

The public's love affair with the Morris Minor began when it made its debut at the first post-war Motor Show at Earls Court in 1948. In the face of stiff opposition from the imposing Jaguar XK120, Morris's new-look small car for the post-war era stole the show. Rave reviews highlighted the Minor's 'new' monocoque construction, complimented the car's compactness, marvelled at its handling and acclaimed the work of designer Alec Issigonis.

For Issigonis, the Turkish-born draughtsman recruited from Rootes Motors in 1936 initially to undertake suspension design, the plaudits provided overdue recognition of his undoubted engineering talent and vindication of his decision to persevere with the innovative features of his design. The latter was a considerable achievement in view of the fact that Lord Nuffield (William Morris) had taken an instant dislike to the car, disparagingly calling it a 'poached egg' when he first viewed a prototype 'Mosquito'. Lord Nuffield also objected to this name, so at his insistance production models were redesignated Morris Minor.

Although Issigonis had been given a free hand to design a new small car and had been successful in ensuring that most of his original ideas were incorporated into the prototypes, some important changes were forced upon him and the other members of his small team, Jack Daniels and Reg Job. The most significant was the decision to retain the Morris 8 Series E's sidevalve engine. Doubts were expressed over the economic sense of producing entirely new engines whose effectiveness was questionable, so the Issigonis-inspired 800cc and

John Ford's 1950 Series MM two-door saloon in Romain Green (above) shows off the original 'low-headlamp' nose and chromed grille. The Morris Minor in its earliest form was praised for its surefooted handling, positive steering and smooth ride. The 5in headlamps seen here were, at best, only adequate.

1100cc water-cooled, flat-four, sidevalve engines were consigned to history after undergoing extensive testing, with mixed results, in the prototype Mosquitos. With them went the original idea of using a bench seat arrangement in the front and a three-speed column gearchange. Instead a more conventional four-speed floor gearchange was adopted along with separate front seats – albeit in a wider body than was originally envisaged.

A famous story relates how, in a momentous eleventh hour decision and on Issigonis's instructions, one of the prototype Mosquitos was sawn in half – lengthways. Mounted on blocks, the halves were moved apart until at four inches, according to an official press release, "proportion was propitiated and harmony satisfied". More than that, "the lines of the Morris Minor

The Series II models, introduced in 1952/53, continued in their early form to share many of the previous Series MM features, but the much-loved Traveller was an addition to the range. All early Series IIs, including the Traveller, retained a painted honeycomb grille panel,

split windscreen and long bonnet. The main external distinguishing feature was a new bonnet badge and motif. This 1953 Traveller belonging to Bryan Gostling is believed to be the earliest surviving example.

were settled and a new breeding line for the small cars from the Nuffield Organisation was founded".

Evidence of this radical decision to widen the car is plain to see on all Morris Minors, for the overall dimensions determined in 1948 remained unchanged throughout production. The extra width added to the body is most obvious on the bonnet, where a 4in central strip is prominent. In addition, early Series MM models, the first Morris Minors to be produced, had split front and rear bumpers and valences, metal fillets bridging the gap.

As for the "new breeding line", mainstream production of two-door saloons and tourers began at Cowley in October 1948. Initial estimates of the Minor's potential sales proved so wide of the mark that new assembly lines had to be set up to cope with the demand. Full order books and a healthy export trade helped ensure the continued development of the cars and contributed to the launch of further new models. The four-door saloon came in 1950, and the Traveller and the light commercial range were announced in 1953.

Assisted by the merger between the Austin Motor Company and the Nuffield Organisation to form the British Motor Corporation, progress continued and a new line in engines, the A-series, took the Minor a major step forward. A radical update in 1956, when the familiar split screen disappeared with the introduction of the popular Minor 1000 models, signalled the start of the boom years, which led in early 1961 to the Minor becoming the first British car to sell one million in all its forms.

With final flurries in development in 1962

An interesting comparison between two of the first-generation Series MM models. This gorgeous Peak District shot clearly shows the differences between an early 'low-headlamp' tourer (a 1949 Maroon car owned by Keith Fletcher) and a late 'high-headlamp' four-door saloon (a 1952 Clarendon Grey car owned by the author). The original design by Alec Issigonis accommodated the change from two to four doors with little modification.

This fine 1955 Series II convertible in Clarendon Grey is owned by Trevor Lammas and has covered just 22,000 miles from new. It illustrates the significance of the Series II's major update in October 1954, when a new grille panel with painted horizontal bars was introduced.

and 1964, the Minor began to drift towards the inevitable end of production, which eventually petered out in 1971 after a staggering 1.6 million had been produced. Production had been concentrated at Cowley, but in later years this extended to Abingdon and Adderley Park, the latter being where Travellers and light commercials were assembled.

Production was not confined to Britain. Completely Knocked Down (CKD) models were assembled in numerous countries throughout the world, contributing to their local economies and at the same time enhancing the reputation of what the marketing department billed the world's supreme small car.

Given that the Morris Minor in all its guises was promoted worldwide and that it fulfilled its promise as a dependable means of transport, it is not altogether surprising that in the post-production years it has continued to attract a new generation of equally enthusiastic followers. For any would-be owner there is a tremendous choice in the models available, some of them, of course, being rare and others more suited in original specification for everyday use.

The earliest Morris Minors, the Series MM models, fall more readily into the realm of collectors' cars rather than cars for everyday motoring. The first MMs, the 1948–50 'low-headlamp' versions, are scarce in the UK owing to the fact that over 75 per cent of them were exported – a quirk of the weak British economy in the post-war years. Of these models, the Series MM tourer is the rarest and the most sought-after. Later 'high-headlamp' two-door and four-door saloons are more plentiful, but still relatively few in number. Although full of character, these original Morris Minors have an inherent weakness in their distinct lack of power. While the moderate acceleration and top speed of 62mph generated by the redoubtable sidevalve engine proved acceptable in the late forties and early fifties, such weak performance becomes a limiting factor in the high-speed world of the nineties.

Series II models, produced between 1953–56 and fitted with the overhead valve engine used in the Austin A30, could only manage 1mph more, although acceleration was improved. In modern everyday motoring they fare little better than the Series MMs, and like their predecessors their original specification trafficators (as opposed to

The arrival of the Morris Minor 1000 in 1956 brought the most well-known production landmark, for a single-pane windscreen replaced the original split design at the same time as a larger 948cc engine was introduced. This superb Clipper Blue two-door saloon is owned by Barry Tibbetts and dates from 1961. Wheels, grille and coachline in correct Old English White complement the body colour to good effect.

flashing indicators) nowadays represent a potential hazard, particularly on motorways.

The versatile ash-framed Traveller was a welcome addition to the Morris Minor range in 1953. Interestingly it entered production a year after the Morris Oxford Series MO Traveller, very much as a scaled-down version. Unlike the Series MO version, the Minor Traveller continued in production until 1971 in updated form, surviving very much against the odds in view of the fact that factory sources show that it cost more to produce than its asking price during the final years. Like the desirable convertible models, the Series II Traveller, easily identified by its split windscreen, is a rare variant.

The Morris Minor 1000 models, which made their debut at the Earls Court Motor Show in 1956, are the first of the Minors which can be viewed as being positively suited to everyday use today in original form. The 948cc overhead valve engine's stronger performance combined with improved gear ratios and a higher back axle ratio to inspire more confidence. Some reservations remain over the trafficators, which were fitted as standard until 1961 on home market models.

The additional improvements which resulted in 1962 from the installation of a 1098cc engine and better braking, along with prominent and more effective combined brake/indicator lamps a year later, helped to maintain the Minor 1000's popularity in its final years, and for many people continue to exert a positive influence

Although the Minor 1000 was given a 1098cc engine for the final major update in 1962, the large indicator/stop/tail lamp units typical of the breed, and seen here, came along a year later. This Smoke Grey four-door saloon owned by Mike Taylor dates from 1966 and has covered just 26,000 miles from new.

Keith Fletcher's 1966 convertible in Almond Green shows how the hoods on later cars adopted a larger rear window in common with saloon versions, but this hood's white colour is a non-standard personal choice. The large indicator/sidelight units seen here are common to all 1098cc models produced after October 1963.

when it comes to deciding which Morris Minor to own now.

The light commercial models are the most versatile variants. Many businesses today nostalgically seek out the few survivors in order to emulate companies of the past which responded to the lure of contemporary advertising and used the van and pick-up models to ply their trade. In keeping with factory practice, some modern day owners still fit their own personalised bodies onto basic chassis/cab structures. Specialist users, such as the Post Office, disposed of their vehicles many years ago, but enthusiasts keen to see these special contract vehicles restored to their former glory research their history in an effort to recreate authentic livery and specification details.

For purists who prefer to see cars used in original specification, life can be difficult. For all its character and charm, the Minor has been for many people a practical and versatile workhorse. As a consequence, cars have been personalised, uprated and modified over the years. In a way, the Minor's progressive development has contributed to this, the increases in engine size, for instance, encouraging owners to replace 'tired' engines with more up to date alternatives. It's not unusual to find sidevalve cars fitted

with overhead valve engines, Series II cars with later 948cc or 1098cc engines and gearboxes, and 1098cc Minor 1000s with larger 1275cc MG Midget or Morris Marina engines. Corresponding amendments to brakes and suspension are commonplace.

Odder modifications can also occur. In Australia, one of the largest export markets and one where the Minor is still held in high regard, the easy availability of Japanese parts means that it's not unusual to find Minors with Datsun 1200 engines and Toyota five-speed gearboxes. Concessions to safety, understandable given some of the drive-ability problems already identified, have also resulted in a variety of non-standard flashing indicator arrangements being installed.

One of the choices facing today's owner is whether to retain the original features of his or her vehicle or forfeit some of them in order to meet the perceived needs of the modern era. For someone contemplating restoration, decisions also have to be made about whether to retain original parts for as long as possible or replace them lock, stock and barrel as part of a full restoration. Ultimately it becomes a matter of personal preference, and more often than not a compromise. Having said that, Morris Minor owners are in a much better position

Introduced in May 1953, the popular light commercial versions continued in production until 1971, combining unique specifications with some of the normal run of car updates. This view of a 1958 Sandy Beige pick-up, owned by Neville Wright and fitted with a period accessory tonneau cover, shows two interesting differences compared with a contemporary car model: the shortened front bumper blade and Series MM style of bonnet badge remained unchanged throughout commercial vehicle production.

Late in commercial vehicle production, from 1968, British Leyland (née BMC) created Austin-badged Series C alternatives of the 8cwt van and pick-up alongside the normal Morris Series V versions. Although its marque identity cannot be spotted from this angle, this 1971 Connaught Green van owned by Neville Wright is badged as an Austin.

to undertake restoration to original specification than many of their counterparts who own other marques and models.

A strong network of parts suppliers and specialist companies has become firmly established in the UK since production ceased, and some body panels are still produced using the original presses. There is a thriving club scene, spearheaded by the UK-based Morris Minor Owners' Club and supplemented by long-established clubs in most of the principal countries in Europe, as well as in the USA, South Africa, Australia and New Zealand.

With luck and good judgement, perhaps in years to come the theme *Original Morris Minor* will extend beyond the title of this book to a greater proportion of the cars which have come to be so highly regarded throughout the world.

MORRIS MINOR SERIES MM (1948-53)

The author's 1952 Series MM four-door saloon, finished in Clarendon Grey, is a two-owner car which has covered just 37,000 miles from new. Standard features on the four-door saloons included chromed over-riders and stainless steel door window surrounds.

The exhibits on the Morris Motors stand at the Earls Court Motor Show in 1948 featured a whole new model range comprising the Morris Six (MS), the Morris Oxford (MO) and the Morris Minor (MM). It is, of course, well-documented that the diminutive Minor two-door saloon and tourer models on display attracted most of the attention, much to the surprise of the Morris Motors management who had high expectations for the Morris Oxford MO.

All the new Morris models adopted the new monocoque method of construction, a significant innovation which on the Morris Minor models was complemented by rack and pinion steering, independent front suspension and new 14in road wheels. A tasteful interior aptly named 'New Note' and a range of bright exterior paint colours brought a bit of sparkle into the austere post-war years, where ration books and petrol coupons were still part of the scene. Unbeknown to the watching public, it was the beginning of a new era in motor car design. History in the making!

BODY & CHASSIS

The Morris Minor Series MM is of monocoque construction. Unlike most pre-war cars which had a separate body and chassis, the new post-war Morris sported an all-steel body with the underframe incorporated as an integral part of a single unit. In 1948 it was a relatively new concept but one destined to catch on throughout the motor manufacturing world.

The importance of understanding the methods used in unitary construction was acknowledged by Morris Motors soon after production of the whole range of monocoque Morris vehicles began. In conjunction with the Pressed Steel Co Ltd and Nuffield Metal Products, they produced a very informative manual, *Morris Mono-Construction* (Morris Motors Publication), to assist those concerned with the rectification of accident damage to Morris cars.

The following summary, which identifies the three main assemblies and their constituent parts, provides an insight into the process of constructing a monocoque body. This was deemed useful at the inception of Morris Minor production for those involved in working with the cars and for overseas assembly plants which imported the body components in CKD (Completely Knocked Down) form and assembled complete cars using some components from their own suppliers. It would seem particularly apt to

Keith Fletcher's 1949 Series MM tourer has been meticulously restored to original specification. It exhibits all the classic features of the early Morris Minor: grille-mounted head-lamps, divided bumpers, split windscreen and chrome-plated grille. The tourer's detachable rear sidescreens allowed the car to be completely open rearwards of the doors, giving true meaning to the phrase 'wind-in-the-hair' motoring for rear seat passengers!

One of the last open-top Series MMs is this 1953 convertible owned by John Gamble. The addition of the fixed sidescreens shown here distinguishes the convertible from the earlier tourer, which had detachable sidescreens.

include an edited version of the text in this publication for those seeking to rebuild a Morris Minor to original specification:

'The mono-construction of the Morris Minor consists of three main assemblies: the forward end assembly, the floor assembly and the outer shell assembly.

'The forward end assembly is built upon two longitudinal members, commonly referred to as front chassis legs. These are bridged at the front by a short crossmember welded between them. The chassis legs also carry the brake pedal boss and clutch relay pivot together with the front suspension reinforcement tubes and front engine mounting brackets. Horizontal tie plate assemblies complete the box sections of the front half of the chassis legs and extend outwards to the inner wheelarch panels. A top plate welded to the front crossmember forms the front end box section. A toeboard panel located behind the toe plates bridges the structure. A single pressing – the bulk-head panel which incorporates a bulkhead crossmember, battery box and shock absorber stiffener brackets – is positioned above the toeboard panel and the two are welded together.

'Both wheelarch panels are welded to the

flanges on the toe plate assemblies, the bulkhead panel, the toeboard panel and the bulkhead crossmember assembly. Brake hose brackets are located near the outside edge of each of the wheelarch panels.

'The front bumper bracket supports are spot-welded in a forward position to the tie plate flanges, while the rear end of each bracket is welded to the wheelarch panel.

'The final parts of the forward end

assembly are the inner side panels, which are spot-welded to the bulkhead panel and the wheelarches. At the rearward end of the front chassis legs the centre crossmember assembly is welded in position.

'The floor assembly has the rear spring brackets, cable clips, hydraulic damper link pins, a shackle tube and spare wheel clamp reinforcement welded to it. The body sills which run along the perimeter of the body

15

This exploded drawing is from the Morris Mono-Construction *manual. It shows the Series MM two-door, but the basic structure remained the same throughout production.*

Key to Body Components
1,2 Door assembly. **3** Trunk lid. **4** Trunk panel. **5** Lower rear squab support. **33, 34** Rear quarter inner panel. **35, 36** Rear wheelarch. **37** Shackle plate and towing eye. **39** Jack plate. **40** Front wheelarch to body side boxing plate. **42** Bracket, trunk opening to floor. **43** Trunk floor support member. **45** Back-light reinforcement.

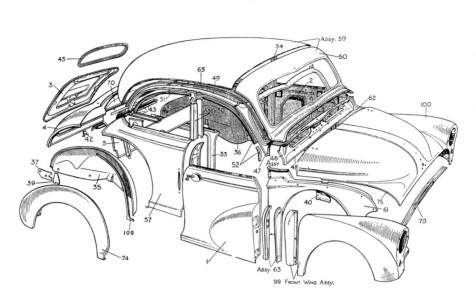

46 Fascia panel. **47** Top portion fascia panel. **48** Lower portion fascia panel. **49** Roof side inner reinforcement. **50, 54** Upper shut pillar. **51** Quarterlight top facing. **52** Door opening top facing. **57** Rear quarter panel. **59** Roof and windscreen opening panel assembly. **60** Windscreen opening panel. **61, 62** Front body side panel. **63** Hinge pillar extension assembly. **65** Drip moulding. **70** Upper rear squab support. **74** Rear wing. **75** Bonnet. **76** Bonnet crossmember. **99, 100** Front wing. **109** Rear wheelarch connecting piece.

between the front and rear wheelarches are riveted as well as being spot-welded to the floor panel. Rivets are also used in addition to welding to secure the rear seat crossmember to the floor. These rivets also pick up the rear spring hanger brackets on the underside of the floor panel. Boxing plates welded along the sill and floor panel flanges form a box section and provide additional strengthening: this is further enhanced with the welding of the ends of the rear seat crossmember to the body sills.

'The process of assembling the outer bodyshell for saloon models commences with the boot/trunk surround panel, the rear quarter panels, the fascia assembly panel, the roof side inner reinforcement rails and the door shut/pillar assemblies being located and clamped together. The boot/trunk surround panel is spot-welded to the rear quarter panels at a depressed joint which is subsequently lead-loaded (loaded with plumber's solder). The door shut pillars (B post), the inner roof reinforcement rails and the quarter light (rear side window) facing panels are then spot-welded to the rear quarter panels. The roof inner reinforcement rails are gas-welded to the top of the inner windscreen reinforcement panel, to the top of the door shut pillars (B posts) and to the inner reinforcement rails of the rear quarter panels. The joints where the roof side reinforcement rails meet the windscreen reinforcement rail/windscreen pillar (top) and where the fascia panel joins it (bottom) are cleaned off, lead-loaded and hand-finished down to the correct contour.

'Following this the roof and windscreen

opening panel assembly is located and welded in position. The outer windscreen opening panel is spot-welded to the inner windscreen reinforcement panel which then forms the upper half of the fascia panel assembly. The roof panel is then welded to the door opening and rear quarter lights and to the boot/trunk surround panel and the rear quarter panels. Assembly of the outer bodyshell is completed by locating the front inner wing flitch panels and gas-welding them to the windscreen opening panel and door facing panels.

'After completion of the body and underframe build-up procedure, the joint which is exposed between the doors and the bonnet is cleaned off, tin-coated and lead-loaded.

'In order to complete the sub-assembly operations, the rear seat squab support assembly is located on the floor assembly and welded to the floor and sill panels.

'The main floor assembly and front end assembly are next clamped together with the rear wheelarch assemblies and rear quarter panels in position. They are then welded along the inner and outer flanges of the longitudinal members (chassis legs) and along the centre crossmember flanges. The front inner panels are welded to the boxing plates which in turn are welded to the sills, quarter panels and floor. The rear wheelarches and rear quarter inner panels are welded to the squab support, sill flanges and the floor before being welded together. The squab support is then gas-welded to the inner reinforcement rails of the rear quarter panel before being welded to the floor

tunnel. The centre crossmember is welded to the floor, the rear flange being gas-welded through the holes provided in the pressing. This assembly is completed when the front toeboard is welded to the floor and the front inner panels are welded to the boxing plates.

'When this stage is finally reached, the outer bodyshell is fitted over the combined floor and front end assemblies. Templates are positioned in the door and quarter rear window light frames and the whole unit is clamped. The body is then welded at the wheelarches and to the inner reinforcement rails, the rear light and front wheelarch reinforcements; the shock absorber pins, hinge pillar top, shackle and jacking plates are welded in position. The shackle brackets are reamed and the door and window openings cleaned and faced. Drip mouldings are spot-welded to the roof side and the windscreen pillars. Finally, the doors, bonnet, wings and boot/trunk lid are fitted and adjusted, and the depressed joints at the windscreen opening panel and above the boot lid are tinned, lead-loaded and cleaned down.'

The procedure outlined here is applicable to all Series MM models. However, there are obvious differences with the tourer (and the later convertible models) and the four-door saloons. In the case of the open cars, additional strengthening was incorporated to compensate for the absence of the roof panel. Extra strengthening panels were spot-welded at either end of the fascia panel and attached to the A post in an effort to prevent scuttle shake. In order to increase the

The classic lines of the early Series MM frontal style show the effects of the decision to widen the car shortly before production. The metal fillet joining the front bumper halves and flat strip along the centre of the bonnet are conspicuous, although at the time the car was announced no-one attached any particular significance to these features.

perimeter rigidity of the tourer and convertible models, extra strengthening was built into the sill area adjacent to the boxing plates and further bracing was provided by a strengthening bracket positioned on the top of the inner sill and welded to the B post.

Most of the panels used in the monocoque construction are common to tourer and saloon models. However, notable exceptions are the rear quarter panels, which differ as they are designed to accommodate the detachable sidescreens fitted to the tourer, and the windscreen panel, which is modified to accommodate the fixings for the hood.

With the introduction of the four-door saloon in October 1950, an additional exterior moulding was incorporated above the boot/trunk surround panel and beneath the rear window. The switch to four doors also necessitated modifications to the B post design, the rear quarter panels, the sill boxing plates and the side floor panels on the underframe. Later, when the short bonnet was discontinued in August 1951 at chassis number 109699 (RHD), all models were converted to the flush-fitting full bonnet which followed the contours of the extended drip moulding adjacent to the front doors – a feature retained on all subsequent models until the end of production.

The original low-headlamp front wings were pressed in 20-gauge steel. They consist of two pressings – a single outer wing panel and an inner back edge panel – and were designed to be bolted onto the body. The two pressings were joined to form one piece when the leading flange of the inner panel was trapped in a turned edge on the outer

The contrast between rear bumpers on early and later Series MMs. Early cars (right, above) have a metal fillet, as at the front, to join the bumper halves, whereas later cars (right, below) have a one-piece bumper which harks back to the earlier fillet arrangement in having two central chrome bolts. The boot handles seen here are the original type fitted to the Series MM, distinguished by an external fixing with two screws. The recessed number plate panel with its curved edges means that replacement period number plates have to be specially shaped. The chrome cover on the Clarendon Grey car's number plate lamp was an accessory available to replace the standard black-painted cover.

The chromed centre pillar, windscreen rubber inserts and retaining finishers enhanced the appearance of the early models. Difficulties can be encountered in locating and rechroming replacement inserts. Note the position of the interior mirror, which screws into the back of the centre pillar. The wipers – not parked in the normal position here – have their blades secured to the arms by rubber fasteners.

The bonnet stay on early Series MMs (below left) incorporated additional support in the form of a chain concealed here beneath a black rubber cover, but later models (below right) had a simplified arrangement without the chain.

wing and then gas-welded. These original type wings are no longer available, but comparable fabricated versions are available (at a price) and are usually made up of five pieces, including the inner back edge panel from later Minor 1000 wings.

The later high-headlamp wings for Series MM cars were manufactured in a similar manner, but have a revised outer pressing and an inner headlamp reinforcement ring spot-welded in place. Authentic high-headlamp wings are easily distinguished by the smooth profile found at the front inner leading edge, whereas later Minor 1000 wings, which can be modified to fit Series MM cars, have a distinctive protruding joint between the headlamp aperture and the inner flange.

Series MM rear wings, distinguished by

their high-cut profile, were also pressed in 20-gauge steel. A flat, narrow, two-piece metal band was spot-welded to the main outer wing pressing in order to create a large inner flange suitable for bolting the wing to the body. On all Series MM cars, body-coloured wing piping was located between all wings and the body.

The boot lid is constructed of a single outer pressing which includes a number plate panel. An inner reinforcement panel provides rigidity and a full-length boot stay, secured by a sprung metal clip, is mounted to it on the left-hand side. On the same side, a boot stay locating bracket is welded to the underside of the inner edge of the boot aperture. The perimeter of this aperture is covered by a boot seal rubber. A black sound deadening panel is fitted to the inside of the

boot lid. Elsewhere in the boot compartment itself, black is a recurring colour: the rear inner wings are painted matt black, the wooden boot floor panels (located by cross-headed screws) are black, and the black felt rear seat backing is visible through the metal rear seat squab support (which is painted body colour).

All Morris Minor doors are made from steel pressings, lap-joined and welded together. The doors were formed in dies and assembled in jigs, so their dimensions are standardised. New doors are no longer available, although a range of repair panels are. On Series MM models, the size of doors is the same for two-door saloon and tourer/convertible models, whereas the front doors of four-door saloons are shorter.

The door hinges are tightened on to

The facility to use a starting handle was a welcome feature of the Series MM.

This angle of a 1949 Series MM with 'low-headlamp' front wings (below) illustrates some unique original features. Note the single black wiper arm and blade, chromed door window surrounds, curved chrome-plated quarterlight catches, and quarterlights without external hinges. The broad coachline seen here has been the subject of much debate, but period publicity film confirms that the first Minors had this full-width style.

This is the original fuel filler cap on Series MMs. A chain fixing replaced this hinged arrangement on later models.

This 1951 'high-head-lamp' saloon (below) shows the early use of a 'short' bonnet and short bonnet hinges. Painted door window frames and quarterlights with an external hinge (just out of shot) were standard on two-door saloons and convertibles of this era. Morris Minor badging has been introduced on the bonnet and wipers are now stainless. The coachline is now of the conventional width.

sliding plates which move easily to allow for adjustment after the bolts securing them have been slackened. Further adjustment of door fit is possible by similar means when the fixing screws are slackened on the spring-loaded door striker plates. With later Series MM models, the same type of adjustment is possible even though pin and socket plates with a modified handle and lock striker assemblies are fitted.

BODY TRIM

Chrome on the Series MM models was used to good effect in highlighting the flowing lines of the body styling. It was, if anything, understated compared with many contemporary models, even some within the Morris range such as the Morris Oxford

This 1952 four-door saloon (left) has the 'long bonnet', revised bonnet hinges, stainless steel door window surrounds and a new style of quarterlight catch. The Morris Minor badging is retained, albeit in a revised position.

The grille panel changed considerably during MM production. The headlamps on the earliest cars (above) are incorporated into the grille panel and the grille itself is chrome-plated. The headlamp adjustment screw can be seen directly beneath the lamp.

'High-headlamp' versions (above) have a revised grille panel which incorporates the separate sidelights, and early models retained a chrome-plated grille. Note the screw fastening on the headlamp rim.

The location of the headlamps on the grille panel on early cars made it necessary for this cover panel (above left) to be fitted in order to link the grille and the inner wing panel. Later transitional vehicles retained this panel (above right), but the absence of low headlamps left an exposed recess, which can be seen on the left of this picture.

A world shortage of nickel in 1951 forced a rethink on chrome items, the change to a painted metal grille (above) being one consequence which remained to the end of Series MM production.

Series MO, with its heavily chromed grille.

The base metal for almost all of the chromed components is Mazak, a widely-used metal of the time which does not withstand the ravages of corrosion particularly well. Its tendency to pit presents problems if original components need to be rechromed owing to the unavailability of original style replacement parts. Significant differences exist in the chrome parts used on different models. Variations in the design of some components and the length of time they were fitted to some models makes the replacement or refurbishment of original parts an interesting, if at times frustrating, part of restoring a Series MM to original specification.

The chromed parts which remained

The painted grille on later Series MMs was generally finished in body colour, but black cars were a special case in having a contrasting grey grille (above), Birch Grey being the shade most frequently used.

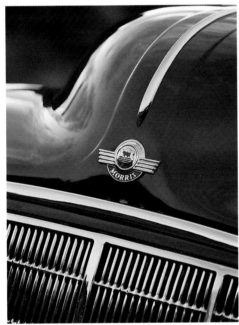

Escutcheon plates were not fitted on the door handles of the early cars, as seen here (above) on the first ever production Morris Minor, registered NWL 576. Following its restoration by BMC apprentices in 1961, this car was painted in its original Platinum Grey but incorrectly given a narrow coachline.

The distinctive Morris badge and bonnet flash (right) as fitted to the Series MM models and subsequently retained on commercial vehicles, a fact which has helped ensure supplies of 'new old stock'.

Door handle escutcheon plates were fitted to later cars, as shown on the rear door of this four-door saloon (above). The moulding on the body was a feature introduced on the four-door bodyshell in 1950 and extended to the rest of the range following the permanent change from 'low-headlamp' to 'high-headlamp'.

The Series MM boot badge is a rare commodity in original form, although reproductions of the casting are available. The original type of reflector shown here has a domed profile and is an elusive item in sound condition.

unchanged throughout Series MM production are the centre windscreen pillar, windscreen rubber chrome inserts and joining pieces, boot badge, boot handle, bonnet flash and bonnet badges. The last two items continued in use after the Series MM ceased production, as well as featuring on all the commercial vehicles and some later export models – this fact has helped to ensure their continued availability. The same cannot be said of the windscreen surrounds, which are in short supply and have to be rechromed. Since these are not Mazak, good results can be achieved in spite of their flimsy construction. The four flat bumper blades fitted to the low-headlamp models, the later one-piece bumpers (introduced in January 1951) along with the front grille insert, and the early type window frames are the only other non-Mazak chromed items.

Door handles differ in style between the later four-door saloons and the earlier two-door saloon and tourer models. Outer escutcheon plates were introduced on the four-door saloon and their use was extended to the two-door and convertible models soon after, at car numbers 69622 (RHD) and 70876 (LHD). They continued to be used on all models until the end of production.

Two types of bonnet hinge were used on Series MM cars. The early short type – which incidentally double as door hinges for some Berkeley three-wheeler models! – were used with all low-headlamp models and some of the transition high-headlamp cars which still used the short bonnet. Unlike the later type of hinge used on Series MM models with long bonnets, and on subsequent cars, the early hinges are not interchangeable.

Series MM boot hinges differ from those used on later models due to the fact that they have a narrower profile and a more pointed bottom end. The boot handle uses an external screw type fixing which distinguishes it as being original to the Series MM,

The wooden floor of the boot and rear inner wings should be painted black. The body coloured boot stay is held in position when the boot is closed by a spring clip on the opposite side of the boot lid.

The spare wheel compartment is also used to stow the tool kit, on the opposite side to the spare wheel; Series MM tourer sidescreens are stored on top of the spare wheel. The boot catch shown here is the type fitted to later MMs and distinguished by its curved profile, a feature which helps to make the locking mechanism more secure.

but it is interchangeable with the later types described in subsequent chapters.

The front panel on the early models housed the headlamps and a separate chrome-plated grille panel. The outer panel was held in place in part by a pair of chrome 'hockey sticks' bolted through the inner edge of the wing, a chrome top grille surround and a series of bolts which located the bottom edge to an inner flange on the body. At first the chrome insert was located by studs on the inside of the panel and secured by a series of push-on clips. When the design of the chrome insert was modified, however, instructions were issued to remove eight of the studs so that the redesigned and extended top edge could fit flush over where the studs had been and be secured along with the outer panel using the top grille bar 2 BA stud and nut arrangement; the four remaining studs were fastened as before. This arrangement superseded the original one as the modified grille insert was issued as a replacement in all cases until a third option became available – a one-piece all-steel pressing for low-headlamp models.

The transition from low-headlamp to high-headlamp meant that for a time the chrome insert was used in the revised panel which had sidelights included. Finally, in late 1951, the chrome insert was replaced by a one-piece steel pressing which was used until the end of production. For all models except those painted black, the panel was painted body colour. On black cars, the actual grille pressing was painted a contrasting grey colour.

The door top assembly on Series MM cars changed significantly between 1948-53. On early saloons and tourers, the door top assembly – including the front quarter light – was chromed. After November 1949 at car number 31781, painted door tops were introduced and these continued in use until 1953. The four-door saloon was fitted with stainless steel door tops, and this was the first model to be fitted with a revised front quarter light assembly catch.

LIGHTING

The lighting arrangements on Series MM models were subject to considerable change. Legislation governing lighting, particularly in the USA, had immediate repercussions for the overall design of the front end of the Series MM Morris Minor and affected the styling of all subsequent models.

The small 5in headlamps fitted in the grille panel of the early cars incorporated a pilot light. Each light unit consists of a lamp glass,

An original Lucas 5in headlamp showing the outer chrome bezel, distinctive diamond shape on the lens and the adjustment screw; one of the side-mounted locating screws can just be seen.

The later 'triangular' stop/tail light showing glass, chrome bezel and body-coloured base. The reflector is an owner-added accessory. It is worth noting the bumper mounting arrangement on split bumper models. The bracket shown here was sandwiched between the body and the inner edge of the wing.

reflector and chrome rim, and is suspended in the grille panel between two rubber bushes and held in position by two screws. A unique feature of these lamps is the fact that they provide illumination under the bonnet when switched on. When supplied originally, home-market models were fitted with double-filament bulbs in the left-hand headlamp. Operation of the dip switch extinguished the right-hand headlamp and simultaneously deflected the left-hand beam downwards and to the left. Export models were fitted with double-filament main bulbs and pilot bulbs in both headlamps, so the operation of the dip switch allowed for the conventional use of the dipped beam system. These original type headlamps are Lucas F575 P/1, of part numbers 50529A (nearside, home), 50537A (offisde, home) or 50529A

(both sides, export). These headlamps are now difficult to obtain and as a consequence it is becoming increasingly common to find restorers having original units resilvered.

The revised lighting arrangement, introduced as early as 1949 for some export models, used separate headlamp and sidelight units. A 7in Lucas F700 headlamp (part number 51336) was held in place by three spring-loaded adjustment screws on the front edge of a backing shell inserted into the top of each wing. A feature of the Series MM units is the external securing screw fitted to the chrome outer rim. Double-filament bulbs were used in the headlamps and this allowed for full use of the dipping mechanism. The separate sidelight units (type 489, part number 52139) positioned on either side of the grille, on the front panel,

Although the early trafficators are full of character and nostalgia, their low position (top) on two-door saloons and tourer/convertible models creates functional shortcomings, exacerbated by erratic operation. A slight improvement in visibility accompanied the higher position adopted on four-door models (above).

A matching hood cover of imperfect fit was supplied as part of the original tourer/ convertible specification for use when the hood is down.

The tourer's detachable sidescreens are located by two metal pins which slot into brackets located on top of the rear quarter panel. The maroon piping featured here is correct for this model.

The distinctive and authentic shape of the rear window on the Series MM hood. Rearward visibility is merely adequate!

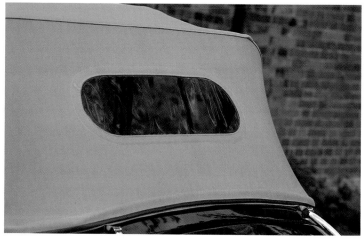

consist of a convex white glass held in place by a chrome retainer pressed into a moulded rubber casing which houses the main body of the lamp.

Rear lamps on the Series MM were also subject to considerable change. In very early cars produced for the home market, a single wing-mounted rear lamp with a central screw was used, supplemented by a reflector fitted in a corresponding position on the other side of the car. This system was then updated to incorporate twin stop and tail lights. Instead of a central screw, the revised units had a glass and a plated rim held in the moulded rim of a rubber surround. It was recommended that home market cars used Lucas double-filament bulb 361 'for a marked increase in brilliance when the brakes are applied'.

The final Lucas type 471 rear lamp unit fitted to the Series MM cars from chassis number 17580 (RHD), in June 1949, has been variously described as the 'shield' type or the 'triangular helmet' type. These were much more effective as lamps and were more prominently mounted on a body-coloured base attached to the wing. The stop/tail lamp bulbs were contained within a moulded glass which was held in place by a chrome bezel secured by two chrome screws.

The Lucas type 467/2 number plate lamp contained two bayonet fitting 6W bulbs (Lucas 989). The outer cover, which fitted over clear glass, was painted black and held in position by a single hexagon screw. Later, outer chrome covers became available and these are often fitted now in preference to the original black-painted ones.

WEATHER EQUIPMENT

A beige canvas waterproofed hood was fitted to all Series MM tourers and convertibles, and tourer models had matching sidescreens. The hood frame was painted black and on early models was made up of four hood sticks and a specially shaped two-piece fabric-covered wooden front rail which was designed to accommodate the profile of the angled split windscreen. A three-piece rear wooden inner rail was screwed to the body behind the rear seat squabs and painted black. Press stud fastenings secured the hood fabric to the body and to the sidescreens. The locating pins on the top of the windscreen and the associated winged bolts on the front rail were chrome-plated. An additional feature of the early hoods was the use of coloured piping for edge trimming, with maroon, green and brown listed as the colours available. Later changes to the hood assembly included an increase in the number of hood sticks from four to five, and the introduction of tension wires for a short period of time. This coincided with the

Extensive use was made of contrasting piping for the interiors of early Series MMs. The maroon piping on these bucket front seats extended to the rear seat and the armrests on the rear quarter trim panel. The moquette-covered rubber door seal required the use of a metal finishing cap, just visible here, on each B post on tourers and convertibles. Note too the integral rubber heel mat in the driver's footwell carpet.

introduction of fixed rear side windows instead of detachable sidescreens at chassis number 100920 (RHD) in June 1951.

Rearward visibility on the Series MM tourer and convertible left something to be desired, so much so that owners have usually sacrificed originality for safety when replacing the hood covering. Such is the rarity of these cars in the UK that templates of the original rear window shape are much sought after by restorers seeking to return their vehicles to original specification.

INTERIOR TRIM

Early sales literature extolled the virtues of the 'natural tones' of the interior trim. This was certainly true on the low-headlamp and 'transition' models, whose beige, brown and gold colourings blended well and created the impression of careful planning and coordination.

A four-piece board-type headlining was fitted as standard to all Series MM saloons, made up of a centre panel, two overlapping side panels and a rear panel fitted underneath the rear window. The early version was covered in a light beige cloth, whereas the later type used a Rexine material available in either dark beige or grey. Sound-deadening underfelt was sandwiched between the headlining boards and the roof, and the three major roof panels were gripped at their outer edges where they came into contact with the front and side inner reinforcement rails and the inner rear window surround. The rear panel and the rear edge of the side panels were secured by self-tapping screws.

Seating in the Series MM cars is functional but comfortable. The bucket front seats have a curved board back panel and the seat base is supported by a series of interlocking springs. The driver's seat can be adjusted by a spring-loaded lever which allows the seat to be moved and then locked in position.

The rear seat comprises a sprung rear seat base and a pivoted rear squab which folds down to provide direct access to the boot compartment. When in the normal upright position, the seat is held in place by a dot and pin fastener positioned underneath the rear window.

The seats, door trims and side panels were originally covered in Vynide leathercloth. Beige was the only colour used until late 1950, when it was supplemented on four-door models by green and brown. However, within the period when beige was the sole colour, there were a number of variations in the use of contrasting seat piping – a table

On later Series MMs, like this 1951 two-door, the use of contrasting piping was restricted to the outer edges of the seat cushions and backrest and to the armrests on the rear quarter trim panel.

This is the original interior of a 1952 four-door saloon. The front seats have leather facings and the rear door pulls/armrests are covered in leather, but the rest of the interior is finished in Vynide leathercloth. The chromed strips on the door trim panels are a feature of four-door models.

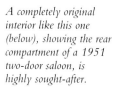

A completely original interior like this one (below), showing the rear compartment of a 1951 two-door saloon, is highly sought-after.

Folding seat backs and tipping seat bases (below) are necessary to provide easy access to the rear on two-door saloons, tourers and convertibles. The simple floor-mounted four-bolt fixing allowed a choice of fixed positions.

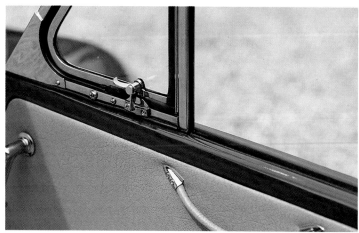

Chromed door window surrounds and curved catches for the opening quarterlights are features of the early Series MM models. The early door pull consists of a wire covered in matching trim material and secured by two chrome-plated end caps held in place by four chromed screws.

The later leather door pull has a chromed metal finisher secured by two chromed screws, concealing the fixing arrangement to the door frame. This four-door model has stainless steel door window surrounds and the later type of quarterlight, subsequently used on all models.

listing the colour combinations appears at the end of this chapter. There was also an evolution in the use of piping on the seats. Early cars had contrasting piping on the outer edges of the front and rear seats, and on the inner edges where the vertical and horizontal panels joined. By late 1949, this pattern had been changed so that the contrasting piping was restricted to the outer edges, and by 1951 the use of contrasting seat piping had been discontinued. With the introduction of the new colours, matching piping was used until the end of Series MM production.

The original type of carpet fitted to the Series MM models was Karvel. As this material is no longer available alternative sources have to be sought, but to date the characteristics of the original type have not been emulated. Carpet colours used in the 1948-53 period were restricted to brown, green and maroon.

In two-door and tourer/convertible models, the carpet set consisted of a one-piece front mat with an integral black rubber heel pad, a one-piece rear mat, two inner sill pieces and two front wheelarch cover pieces. Underfelt was placed loosely beneath each mat and secured to each wheelarch by two screws. The carpet was held to the floor by Veltex fasteners. In addition to being glued down, the top edge of the silver-coloured kick plates helped to locate the carpet covering the inner sills. On early models these kick plates were in unpainted aluminium, but later they were made of steel and painted silver.

This is the correct brown appearance for the steering wheel boss on early Series MM cars. These instruments remained in use throughout Series MM production. The gear lever knob is the correct type for this car.

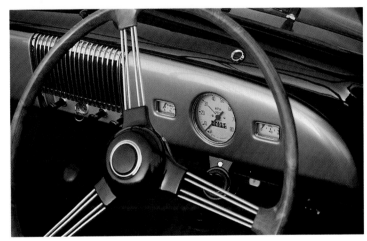

The carpet set fitted to the four-door saloons varied slightly in that the rear carpet consisted of separate right-hand and left-hand pieces, as well as a shaped tunnel cover which took account of the ashtray mounting bracket and the handbrake assembly. Additional trimming pads included matching front wheelarch side panels and a cover panel on the front edge of the rear seat mounting panel.

Door sealing rubbers changed during production. Sorbo sealing rubbers were used on early cars, but this material was discontinued within the first year of production and replaced by the more aesthetically pleasing clip-on, moquette-covered door sealing rubber. Romain Green, Maroon, Grey, Fawn and Empire Green colours of this material were used as appropriate to complement the interior colour scheme.

DASHBOARD & INSTRUMENTS

The Series MM fascia panel is simplistic in its styling and layout. On the early cars, a centrally placed grille with polished Mazak slats, backed by a contrasting mottled black cardboard panel, is flanked by two vertical chrome strips and two gold-coloured cover panels. One of these gold-coloured panels is a hinged glove locker lid released by a press button on top of the fascia, and incorporating a badge (metal up to April 1952, plastic thereafter) displaying the Morris motif. On the driver's side, the other panel contains the Smiths instruments, with the speedometer directly ahead of the driver, flanked by separate gauges for petrol and oil pressure.

Each of these instruments has a cream-coloured face with brown markings. The

The later dashboard layout for Series MMs featured a swivel ashtray in the central grille and lettered pull switches. The additional control beneath the dashboard is a period windscreen washer push.

This trafficator switch (right) is the type fitted to two-door saloon and tourer/convertible models. It is mounted on the strengthening panel which was incorporated into the bodyshell of open cars to provide added strength and prevent scuttle shake.

Viewed from another angle, this shot of the later dashboard shows the mounting arrangement for the trafficator switch on four-door saloons. Unlike the type fitted to two-door saloon and tourer/convertible models, this switch has a timing mechanism which allows the trafficator to self-cancel. Note that part of the steering wheel centre is painted gold on later Series MMs.

speedometer – optimistically marked to record speeds in excess of 80mph! – has a red needle. Within the speedometer, a five-figure odometer records the mileage with white numbers on a black background. An additional feature of the speedometer is a painted red line to indicate the position of the needle at 30mph. The petrol gauge, rectangular and partly concealed by the cover panel, is marked in quarterly increments. The oil pressure gauge, round and also partly concealed, indicates up to 80lb psi with increments of 0-20-40-60-80.

The pull switches for the choke, lights and starter, along with the ignition key, are located directly beneath the centre panel. The backing panel, coloured silver, provides a contrast for the brown Bakelite switches, which are plain and unlettered on early cars. The wiper pull switch, positioned centrally on top of the fascia above the centre panel,

A metal insert placed on top of the windscreen rubber was screwed to the inside of the windscreen frame on some of the *earliest Series MMs. A similar arrangement was employed for the rear screen.*

The spacious engine bay of the Series MM housing the 918cc sidevalve engine in its early form. Features worthy of note include the integral dynamo-mounting bracket, the absence of any heating apparatus, the correct adjustable wire clips for the radiator hoses, and the early type of radiator cap.

is activated when the ignition is switched on by being pulled upwards.

The starter pull switch, positioned to the extreme right of the control panel, is operated by being pulled firmly outwards and then released quickly when the engine fires. The choke control, on the extreme left, is operated by being pulled out and locked in position after being turned through 90°.

A similar action applies to the headlamp and sidelamp switch located to the right of the ignition switch. Side and tail lamps and the rear number plate illumination light are switched on when the switch is pulled out to its first stop. Provided the instrument panel switch is on, panel lamps (and a green warning lamp) will operate and indicate that the side lamps are on. With a twist to the right and a further pull, the headlamps are switched on.

From early 1950, the control switches were identified by white letters, in December 1951 an ashtray was added to the central fascia panel, and in early 1952 a headlamp main beam warning light was introduced. This was positioned behind the slatted grille in the centre of the fascia, and its colour, unusually, was red.

Additional items on the fascia include an ignition warning light positioned directly above the speedometer. A trafficator switch is positioned just below the driver's end of the fascia panel. On two-door saloon and tourer/convertible models, a brown switch with a red illuminated warning light was fitted, this newer type of switch having to be switched on and off by the driver. Four-door saloons were fitted with another type of switch mounted differently in the same area and easily identified by its white lever. This version lacked a warning light but did incorporate a time switch – so the later Series MM four-door saloons have self-cancelling trafficators.

The ignition key was unusual from 1951 in that it was supplied clipped inside a leather cover. This single key (type FA) operated the ignition, right-hand door and boot lid. Prior to this, two identical keys (type MRN) were supplied on a key ring.

ENGINE

The 918cc sidevalve engine which powered all Series MM cars was an updated version of the unit used in the Morris 8 Series E. This original engine had the identification code USHM, so the version initially fitted to the Morris Minor was coded USHM 2. This robust four-cylinder engine with a 57mm bore and 90mm stroke is capable of producing a modest 27.5bhp at 4400rpm. The firing order is 1-3-4-2.

The cast-iron block and cylinder head, along with the alloy sump, were painted grey on the majority of cars. However, some cars were originally supplied with engines painted in light blue, others were finished in red, and towards the end of production green was introduced. Lack of adhesion of the paint applied to the alloy sump has resulted in some restorers leaving the sump unpainted. Evidence from early photographs and workshop manuals supports the view that this item was originally painted.

The crankshaft of the Series MM engine is carried in three steel-backed white metal bearings which are renewable, while the centre bearing is flanged to take the thrust. The connecting rod big end bearings are also renewable white metal-lined, steel-backed bearings fitted without shims. The small end bearing is of the split type with a clamp bolt and spring washer which enables it to grip the gudgeon pin solidly. The tin-coated aluminium pistons are fitted with two compression rings and one oil control ring.

The camshaft runs in three bearings direct in the cylinder block and these are pressure-fed with oil from the main gallery. Driven from the crankshaft by a duplex roller chain utilising two steel gears, the camshaft operates the valves through the medium of barrel tappets sliding directly in the block. Access to the tappets for adjustment is gained quickly by removing a cover located on the

A detail shot of the dynamo-mounting arrangement on early cars, showing the separate bracket fastened to the integrally-cast extension piece on the cylinder head.

An external oil filter was a late addition to the sidevalve engine, but, as in this case, it would generally be fitted to earlier versions. Indeed, reconditioned units were fitted with this type of filter retrospectively.

left-hand side of the engine. The recommended clearances are .017in (.43mm) hot and .018in (.46mm) cold.

Lubrication on the Series MM engine is by a gear type oil pump located in the sump and driven by a helical gear on the camshaft. On early cars the oil is filtered by a large gauze filter also located in the sump; oil is drawn through this and passed up the pump to connect with a horizontal oil gallery running from the front to the back of the engine. From engine number 63276, an external oil filter of the renewable element type was fitted to the left-hand side of the block. With this type of fitting, the pump is connected to the filter intake and the filter outlet is connected to the oil gallery. The detachable main body of the external oil filter was painted the same colour as the engine, although the top retained its natural metal finish.

Additional external features include the oil filler pipe, which is located adjacent to he dipstick mounting point on the right-hand side of the engine block. It is worth noting that variations exist in the oil filler caps used. Although the basic design of the filler cap remained constant, two different types of metal discs were riveted to the top. The early grey-painted version had a plain disc riveted to the top or the word NOL (a Duckhams brand name) embossed directly on to the top of the filler cap. Later versions used a cream-coloured disc bearing the names of leading lubricant suppliers.

During the course of production, two types of cylinder head were fitted to the Series MM engine and are most easily distinguished by the dynamo mounting brackets. On early cylinder heads, the dynamo mounting bracket is located beneath an extension piece which is an integral part of the casting. From engine number 77001, the cylinder head was modified to accommodate a revised thermostat housing, the fitting of a heater control valve and a revised dynamo mounting bracket arrangement. Instead of the integral casting in the cylinder head, a separate side-mounted bracket was incorporated and the additional bracket used in the earlier cars was dispensed with. The engine block was also modified to allow for the fitting of a front-mounted external water pump, engine type becoming USHM 3.

For those models where a heater was fitted, a blanking plate and drain tap were fitted on the right-hand side of the block where previously the bottom radiator hose had been attached. This was a direct consequence of the extensive re-routing of pipes and hoses associated with the operation of the heater. A measure of the differences between the early and late engines is the number of components listed for each (144 for the early engine without a heater and 228 for models with a heater), a fact which contributed to the use of the designation USHM 3 for these later engines.

Engine ancillaries such as the starter motor and dynamo were supplied by Lucas. Two types of dynamo were fitted, but these are interchangeable. On early cars a C39PV (service number 22250F) was fitted while later cars had a C39PV2 (service number 22258A). The same M35G (service number 25022) starter motor was used throughout. The finish on the main casing (yoke) of these components was normally black, but end plates retained a metal finish. The fan blades, located by four bolts to the dynamo pulley, were painted black, as were the engine mounting turrets which were bolted through the tie plates.

It is worth noting that some of the Lucas components on the engine were date-stamped on the yoke and had the identification codes marked on too. This information provides an additional means of identifying the suitability of such components for particular models.

COOLING SYSTEM

The cooling system employed in the Series MM is of the pressurised thermosyphon variety in which the circulation of water is dependent upon its temperature. Cool water enters the engine via the bottom hose, is heated by the combustion, and subsequently rises through the engine to leave via the top hose, from where it travels down the radiator tubes and is cooled by air drawn into the radiator with the help of the fan attached to the dynamo pulley. The main principle underpinning the success of this system is the location of the radiator header tank well above the top of the engine – a feature clearly demonstrated on the Series MM cars.

The radiator supplied by the Morris

Radiators branch of Morris Motors was painted black and on early cars had a 4lb sq/in round radiator cap. Later cars used a winged cap of similar pressure. The radiator was fitted with a drain tap and a metal overflow pipe. Early Series MMs did not have a water pump and consequently no heater was fitted. However, from engine number 77001 it was possible to fit a water pump, so as a consequence a Morris Minor Car Heater and Water Pump kit (part number 300553) became available in late 1950, using a Smiths recirculatory heater.

FUEL SYSTEM

The petrol tank situated in the boot compartment has a capacity of 5 gallons. It was painted black and located in position by self-tapping screws. A type L SU electric pump, bolted on the side of the battery tray, delivers fuel to a type H1 SU horizontal carburettor. A large and imposing air silencer assembly positioned at a slightly inclined angle was fitted to home-market models, but all export models had an oil-bath AC type of air cleaner. Both types were painted black.

In conjunction with other updates introduced at engine number 77001, the carburettor assembly was amended and slightly repositioned to counter earlier problems of fuel vaporisation, but still retained the designation H1.

EXHAUST SYSTEM

The exhaust fitted to the sidevalve models was originally a three-piece mild steel system comprising a downpipe from the exhaust manifold, an oval-shaped silencer box located immediately below the front passenger floor, and a long rearward tail piece which was shaped to go over the top of the rear axle. The most unusual feature of the system was the incredibly small 1in bore of the end section. An asbestos heat shield was fitted to the underside of the front passenger floor immediately above the silencer box. This feature carried forward to other Morris Minor models, but the panel is longer on Series MMs.

The exhaust was mounted by two canvas-covered rubber straps bolted to the body at one end and connected to adjustable steel exhaust clamps at the other. The front of the exhaust was secured to the cast-iron manifold by means of two bolts which located a sealing gasket between two matching flanges. Steel clamps secured the respective pipes at their junction with the silencer box. The exhaust manifold originally had a matt black finish.

An unusual view of the underside of an early Series MM showing the split-casing rear axle, the floor pressings and the central crossmember.

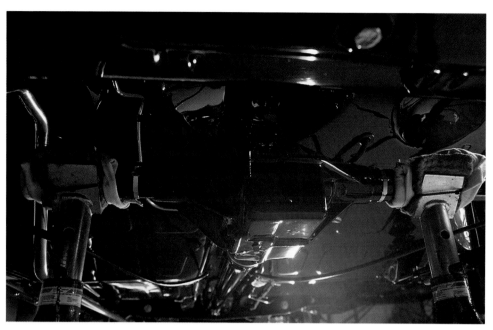

The Armstrong lever arm shock absorber at the rear, complete with mounting bracket. Also visible is the bump stop rubber mounted on the rear axle.

ELECTRICS

From the outset, the electrical equipment on the Morris Minor was 12-volt, incorporating a constant voltage control for the charging system and using positive earth wiring. The battery, originally Lucas BTW7A, a black rubber-cased type with external lead straps linking the cells, was mounted on a tray on the bulkhead under the bonnet. The wiring harness had braided and lacquered inner cables enclosed in an outer black cotton braid with a red stripe.

Two types of Lucas voltage regulator control box were used on Series MMs. The early one had spare fuses carried in clips on the underside of the brown Bakelite regulator cover, while the later one was used in conjunction with a separate fuse holder conveniently positioned immediately beneath the control box.

The ignition system utilised a Lucas

DKYH4A distributor (service number 40056) and a Lucas Q12 ignition coil (service number 45020). The Champion spark plugs were type L10 with a 14mm screw thread and a ½in reach.

On home-market models, a single Lucas HF1235 Windtone horn (service number 069399) was bolted through the tie plate on the right-hand side of the engine, and operated by the horn push in the centre of the steering wheel. The wiper motor was located behind the fascia panel. Initially only one wiper was fitted, but a kit enabling an extra wheelbox to be fitted became available as an optional extra before the two-wiper assembly became standard at car number 72985 (RHD) in late 1950.

TRANSMISSION

Power is delivered by a 6¼in (158.7mm) Borg & Beck single-plate clutch accommodated

within a cast-iron bellhousing which on Series MM cars was painted the same colour as the engine block. The clutch release mechanism is operated by a graphite thrust release bearing located in a fork securely attached to the clutch shaft which itself is connected to the clutch pedal via a lever and operating rod. Adjustment is possible via an adjusting nut on the operating rod.

A four-speed gearbox, very similar to that fitted to the Morris 8 Series E, is used on all Series MM models. Synchromesh operates on second, third and top gear. Even though there is no synchromesh on first or reverse gears, this unit has proved to be very durable and relatively trouble free. The gear ratios are effective, even if the 'box has sometimes to be used vigorously to maintain speed. The ratios are: first, 3.95:1; second, 2.3:1; third, 1.54:1; top, 1.00:1; reverse, 3.95:1. Like the bellhousing, the rest of the gearbox casing was painted the same colour as the engine.

The Hardy Spicer propeller shaft, painted black, has a universal joint at each end consisting of four needle roller bearing assemblies, two yokes and a centre spider. The forward-facing joint is a splined sliding unit which takes account of rear axle movement. There are three lubrication points on the propeller shaft – one for each of the universal joints and one for the sliding joint.

The Series MM rear axle is a semi-floating type with a 4.55:1 ratio. It is distinguished by its divided main casing and integral hub and brake assembly. Its unitary design represented something of a departure for Morris Motors, for the halfshafts, unlike previous Morris models, can only be withdrawn after the wheel hubs, brake drums and brake back assembly plates have been removed. Repairs other than those associated with the halfshafts, wheel bearings and brake assembly can only be carried out when the axle is removed from the car. Final drive is by hypoid final reduction gears. A removable circular cover located in the rear floor pan underneath the rear seat base provides access to the lubrication filler point on the rear axle. In keeping with most of the other rear suspension components, the axle casing, brake backing plates and the exterior of the rear brake drums were painted black. A little-known feature of the Series MM rear axle is the presence of a small breather hole of approximately 1/32in diameter, positioned on the top of the nearside axle casing about an inch from the crown wheel and pinion casing. It is important that this aperture is left clear.

SUSPENSION

The design of the front suspension on the Series MM models caused a great deal of comment among the road test fraternity in the late 1940s. It is a measure of the success of the system employed that its basic design remained unchanged throughout the history of the Morris Minor.

The independent front suspension system has long torsion bars which run either side of the front chassis legs. At the front end each torsion bar is splined into the inner end of the bottom wishbone, and at its rear end each bar is splined into a short lever which can be adjusted to alter the 'trim' of the car. A kingpin is carried in swivel links attached to the top and bottom wishbone arms. The top wishbone arm also serves as the shock absorber link, the shock absorber itself being mounted on specially designed brackets adjacent to the bulkhead. Short, diagonal, rubber-bushed tie rods are fitted between the bottom wishbones and the body.

Almost all the front suspension components were painted black. The exceptions are the torsion bars, which were painted silver, and the unpainted main body of each Armstrong double-acting hydraulic shock absorber, although the shock absorber link was painted black.

The rear suspension utilises semi-elliptic leaf springs with moulded rubber packings fitted on the top and bottom of each spring. The springs are attached to the rear axle casing by U bolts – two on each spring – and are located at the front and rear in rubber bushes. At the front the springs are attached

This view of the front suspension shows the kingpin and the arm to the bulkhead-mounted lever arm shock absorber passing through the inner wing. The steering rack is just visible to the right of the kingpin. The brake drum should be painted black.

This view of a rear spring shows the rear mounting point and the seven spring leaves. The welded plate forward of the rear mounting point is the rear jacking point for the screw jack. The bump stop rubber on the rear axle is visible. The brake drum should again be painted black.

solidly to the body, while swinging shackles are used at the rear. The Armstrong hydraulic rear shock absorbers are bolted to rear spring brackets and to the body via a bushed linking arm. Once again, all the components are painted black with the exception of the main body of each shock absorber.

STEERING

The rack and pinion steering gear is secured to the bulkhead immediately above the clutch bellhousing. Tie rods, operating steering arms, are attached to each end of the steering rack by ball joints enclosed in concertina-type rubber gaiters. The rack itself is painted black. The steering column, brown on the earliest cars but later painted gold to tone in with the rest of the Series MM fascia, engages with the splined end of a helical-toothed pinion to which it is secured by a clamp bolt. End play of the

pinion is eliminated by adjustment to shims fitted beneath the pinion tail end bearing. A damper pad inserted beneath the steering rack controls the backlash between the pinion and the rack. Lubrication to the rack is effected via a lubrication point provided at the left-hand end of the rack housing, which is reached by lifting the front carpet.

The turning circle of the Series MM is 33ft 1in (right-hand lock) or 33ft 11in (left-hand lock). The 16in diameter steering wheel with three spokes, each comprising four chromed steel wires, has a central horn push. In keeping with the steering column, the centre boss was painted brown on early cars and gold on later ones. The moulded rim of the steering wheel provides useful grip on the underside, and was available in a number of attractive colours which complemented the rest of the interior – mottled brown and grey were the most common.

'Low-headlamp' Series MMs had a distinctive line painted on the wheels and were fitted with plain hub caps (right), whereas 'high-headlamp' models dispensed with the line and had hub caps with an M motif (below).

The low-slung nature of the rear leaf springs is accentuated by the high-cut rear wings used on Series MMs (above).

BRAKES

The braking system incorporates Lockheed hydraulically operated brakes on all four wheels with two leading shoes on the front, leading and trailing shoes on the rear. The foot-operated brake pedal is directly linked to the master cylinder mounted in the right-hand chassis leg.

A combination of steel brake pipes, unions and flexible brake hoses link the master cylinder and the wheel cylinders, which are mounted vertically on backing plates. Each brake shoe on the front has a separate wheel cylinder (Lockheed 30357 RH, Lockheed 30358 LH), thus providing the two leading shoes. On the rear wheels a single cylinder (Lockheed 30359) operates both hydraulically and mechanically. Although the type 30359 cylinder originally fitted is very difficult to obtain, Lockheed's later 34577 version is identical except for the addition of an O ring seal on the outer piston.

The handbrake, positioned between the front seats, uses a conventional ratchet and pawl locking device. It operates independently from the hydraulic system through a mechanical cable linkage, the shoes being operated through levers fitted in the brake backplates.

WHEELS & TYRES

The 14in Series MM wheels, specially commissioned from Dunlop, were one of the innovative features much talked about when the Morris Minor was introduced. Revolutionary they may have been – unique they still are. They are not interchangeable with the wheels fitted to later Series II or Minor 1000 models.

The pressed steel rims were fitted with 5.00-14 Dunlop tyres and had four-bolt fixings. On all models the wheels were painted body colour, but on the low headlamp models this was supplemented by a coachline – always in pale cream – on each wheel to match the main coachline painted on either side of the car.

An additional identical feature for Series MM wheels is a three-pin fixing for the hub caps. Plain chrome-plated hub caps were fitted to all models up to early 1951. During the period March to September 1951, a nickel shortage resulted in a temporary halt in the use of chrome-plated grille panels and hub caps, so painted hub caps, at first in plain black and then later in black with an embossed M, were used instead. Following the resumption of normal manufacture, chrome-plated hub caps embossed with the M motif were used until the end of production.

The spare wheel is located under the floor of the boot compartment and on top of the fuel tank. It is held in place with a black-painted wheel clamp, which is secured by an unpainted hexagon bolt located in a specially welded angled support bracket integral to the floor assembly. The retaining bolt can be removed using the wheel brace supplied as part of the tool kit.

The recommended tyre pressures for the Series MM models are 22lb sq/in front and rear in normal use, or 24lb sq/in rear when laden.

TOOL KIT

Series MM models were supplied with a very comprehensive tool kit, which should be stored in the boot in the area between the petrol filler pipe and the body side. The following items were included in the tool roll: screw-type jack, tommy bar (9in), Tecalemit grease gun, tyre pump, wheel brake and hub cap lever, set of BSF box spanners (¼in and ⁵⁄₁₆in, ⅜in and ⁷⁄₁₆in, ½in and ⁹⁄₁₆in), set of double-ended spanners (³⁄₁₆in and ¼in, ¼in and ⁵⁄₁₆in, ⅜in and ⁷⁄₁₆in), screwdriver, distributor screwdriver and gap gauge.

Two types of roll were supplied with Series MM cars. On earlier models a black heavy-duty fabric tool roll with integral pockets and matching ties was used. On 1952 and 1953 models a brown plastic open tool roll with matching cloth ties was supplied.

On the Series MM tourer, a special black cover with two separate compartments was supplied for storing the detachable side screens. It was recommended that the screens should be stored separately to avoid unnecessary damage and that when put in the cover supplied they should be placed on top of the spare wheel.

EXPORT VARIATIONS

Export variations on the early Series MM cars were confined mainly to the essential elements of left-hand drive or right-hand drive steering, mph or kph speedometers and the use of double filament headlamp bulbs.

Most of the other minor changes that occurred relate to the electrical and lighting systems. Whereas the dipswitch on right-hand drive cars is placed high on the toeboard beneath the parcel shelf just to the left of the clutch pedal, for left-hand drive

A full tool kit (above) complete with driver's handbook and period sales literature. The tool roll is a reproduction item.

This is the screw jack in use at the front of the car. Also shown is the combined wheel brace and hub cap remover, along with the tommy bar.

Series MM wheels are distinguished by their three-pin fixing for the hub caps and an aperture which allows brake adjustment with the wheel in place (above).

it was moved to the extreme left of the floor area immediately in front of the driver's seat, requiring the driver to bring his left foot back from the pedals and depress the mechanism with his heel.

Changes to American lighting regulations in 1949 had a significant impact, not only in the specification for lighting arrangements but also for the overall design of the Morris Minor. The requirement for headlamps to sit above a certain minimum height at first resulted in some North American models having a unique specification. They were fitted for the first year with the restyled 'high-headlamp' front wings and revised grille panel housing separate sidelights, but the original split bumper and valance with central metal fillet was retained – an interim arrangement not seen in other markets. After 1950, all 'high-headlamp' models received the one-piece bumpers. Rear stop/tail lights were also modified, and North American cars between car numbers 6142 and 7967 had pedestal-mounted rear lamps.

When the four-door Series MM saloon was introduced in 1950, it was available for export only at first. Additional features of the early export models included a chrome-plated insert in the rear screen rubber and door-mounted ashtrays. The four-door model was also used later in 1952 for preliminary testing of flashing indicators, a feature which replaced the home market trafficators for all North American models from car number 174443 LHD. Other features of all export models included the use of twin horns, an oil bath air filter and an export specification battery.

IDENTIFICATION, DATING & PRODUCTION

The main identification plate – commonly referred to as the chassis plate – is located on the right-hand side of the bulkhead near the wiring harness. It is secured by four self-tapping screws and supplemented by a smaller separate patent plate fixed by two self-tapping screws. During the course of Series MM production, two types of identification plates were used. The early variety displayed a model/type code, the car number and the engine number. From April 1952, a more detailed car number code was used along with the engine number, but the model/type code was discontinued.

The model/type identification code used

These are the first type of chassis and patent plates (right) used on the Morris Minor. The prefix to the car number denotes that this car is a Series MM.

The chassis number was stamped into the bulkhead (below) in the position shown here on all Series MM models. Note also the different location for the coil on this 1952 model.

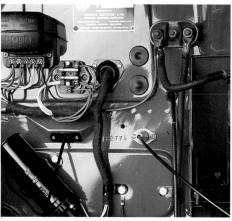

on the early style of plate for Series MM Morris Minors was MNR. An additional code was added to this depending upon the paint finish used: for cars which were finished in Synobel paint the symbol S was used, while for cars finished in Synthetic paint the letters SYN were used. Cars finished in Cellulose enamel were not given an identification code.

The car (chassis) number which was stamped on the main body of the car on the bulkhead was also put on the chassis plate for easy reference and was prefixed with the letters SMM. From April 1952, car (chassis) numbers were prefixed by a new and more detailed identification code consisting of three letters and two numbers, as follows:

First letter Indicates make and model, always **F** for Morris Minor.
Second letter Indicates body style: **A** for four-door saloon, **B** for two-door saloon or **C** for convertible (tourer).
Third letter Indicates the colour in which the car is finished: **A** is Black, **B** is Grey, **C** is Red, **D** is Blue and **E** is Green.
First number Indicates the class to which the car belongs: **1** is RHD home market, **2**

is RHD export, **3** is LHD export, **4** is North American export, **5** is RHD CKD and **6** is LHD CKD.
Second number Indicates the type of paint used: **1** is Synthetic, **2** is Synobel and **3** is Cellulose. At this time all cars in practice were finished in synthetic paint.

Using this code, it can be deduced that a vehicle with the prefix FBB41 would be a Morris Minor two-door saloon finished in grey synthetic paint manufactured for the North American market.

A further identification plate is located in the engine compartment on the left-hand tie plate between the radiator and the inner wing. The body number assigned by Nuffield Metal Products is stamped on a plate welded to the tie plate. This number remains separate from the car (chassis) number and is not recorded on the chassis plate.

The following list provides a quick-reference dating schedule by chassis number for Series MM cars (RHD cars only until April 1952, both LHD and RHD thereafter:

1243 RHD	1 January 1949
4591 RHD	1 April 1949
18491 RHD	1 July 1949
26061 RHD	1 October 1949
33375 RHD	1 January 1950
46415 RHD	1 April 1950
57587 RHD	1 July 1950
63829 RHD	1 October 1950
79783 RHD	1 January 1951
90398 RHD	1 April 1951
106124 RHD	1 July 1951
116618 RHD	1 October 1951
127712 RHD	1 January 1952
139439	1 April 1952
151649	1 July 1952
163401	1 October 1952
175544	1 January 1953

SERIES MM PRODUCTION FIGURES

	Two-door saloons	Tourers	Four-door saloons	Total
1948	1120	52	–	1172
1949	20747	7813	–	28560
1950	?	?	?	48435
1951	25353	6406	16531	48290
1952	25280	6350	14010	45640
1953	?	?	?	3905
Total	?	?	?	176002

Note

A production breakdown for the individual body styles is not possible for 1950 and 1953.

OPTIONAL EXTRAS & ACCESSORIES

Optional extras on Series MM models were kept to the absolute minimum. Initially the only extra was an HMV radio, although after engine number 77007 a heater could be specified on home market models. A popular option featured on several of the cars in this book was a Smiths clock, which matched the speedometer and was fitted to the glovebox lid in place of the Morris badge.

Accessories supplied by Morris dealers included wing mirrors, a travel rug with a prominent Morris emblem, an electric front screen heater/demister, and a unique (and now highly collectible) commemorative battery-powered Victory scale model of the two-door saloon with illuminating headlights.

During Series MM production a number of special non-factory options were offered. Owing to the sidevalve engine's relatively low power output, it was perhaps predictable that some special tuning or engine conversion choices would become available. Three were offered: a Shorrocks supercharger, a 'Silvertop' Derrington conversion and an Alta overhead valve conversion.

The Shorrocks was the most expensive at £80, but *Light Car* were nevertheless mightily impressed when they road-tested a standard sidevalve Minor fitted with the blower. Corrected speeds of up to 80mph were recorded and sports car handling and performance were experienced.

The Derrington 'Silvertop' conversion was endorsed by none other than Stirling Moss, who fitted it to his Series MM to "give it a bit more steam". The full kit comprised an alloy cylinder head (hence the name 'Silvertop'), twin carburettors, special plugs,

This Smiths clock, featured in several of the Series MMs in this chapter, was a popular accessory. It replaced a Morris motif badge, made of metal on early models and plastic on later ones.

This overhead valve conversion, a specialist tuning option supplied by the Alta Engineering Company, boosted the lacklustre performance of the Series MMs.

inlet valve springs, exhaust valves, a Derrington exhaust manifold and a deep-note exhaust system. To complete the effect, a special gear lever extension and wood-rim Derrington steering wheel were fitted. Acceleration was much improved and a top speed of over 75mph was possible.

Perhaps the most comprehensive conversion was that supplied by the Alta Engineering Company. At £45 complete, it was an attractive proposition when *The Motor* road-tested it in 1955, and it remains much sought-after today. The cylinder head, which is cast in aluminium, carries a single line of inclined overhead valves with dual springs, operated by pushrods and forged rockers from the tappets of the original sidevalve engine. Inserted Brico valve seatings are used and the inlet valve diameter is increased by 2mm. The head is designed with siamesed inlet ports so that the normal sidevalve inlet and exhaust manifolds bolt straight to it. The only changes necessary are a short exhaust pipe extension and a different

needle in the SU carburettor. Overall performance with the Alta head fitted is markedly improved, with a top speed of 75mph easily accomplished.

Other non-factory options were specifically aimed at owners of tourers and convertibles. Jarvis and Sons Ltd of Wimbledon offered a 'coupé' conversion with a specially designed hood in 1949 at a cost of £21; a rear screen 'glass' could be fitted on request. It was also possible to convert your tourer or convertible into a saloon – a strange idea when the trend is for the reverse to happen today. Airstream offered a hardtop roof for use on convertibles and ironically enticed owners by suggesting that they could increase the value of a convertible by turning it into a saloon. How times change!

A further optional extra which proved popular with American owners allowed for the fitting of rear wheel 'spats'. These metal covers enclosed the rear wheels and had a dramatic visual effect.

COLOUR SCHEMES (SERIES MM MODELS)

Paint	Trim Two-door/tourer	Trim Four-door	Carpets (all models)
Sep/Oct 1948 to Sep 1950			
Black	Beige/Brown piping	–	Brown
Platinum Grey	Beige/Brown piping	–	Brown
Romain Green	Beige/Green piping	–	Green
Maroon	Beige/Maroon piping	–	Maroon
Sep 1950 to Oct 1951			
Black	Beige/Brown piping	Brown	Brown
Gascoyne Grey	Beige/Brown piping	Brown	Brown
Mist Green	Beige/Green piping	Green	Green
Thames Blue	Beige/Green piping	Green	Green
Oct 1951 to Jun 1952			
Black	Red	Red	Maroon
Gascoyne Grey	Beige	Brown	Brown
Mist Green	Beige	Green	Green
Thames Blue	Beige	Green	Green
Jun 1952 to Feb 1953			
Black	Maroon	Maroon	Maroon
Clarendon Grey	Maroon	Maroon	Maroon
Empire Green	Green	Green	Green
Birch Grey	Maroon	Maroon	Maroon

Notes

The type of paint used on Series MM cars changed early in production. Cars were finished in cellulose prior to 2117 (RHD) and 5855 (LHD) on two-door saloons and 3871 (RHD) and 6255 (LHD) on tourers. Cars after this were finished in either Synthetic or, for a short time, Synobel paint. The original paint finish for each vehicle is indicated in the identification code, details of which appear earlier in this chapter. Relatively few cars were finished in maroon during 1948-50, problems with fading and oxidising leading to its discontinuation. However, this colour was briefly reintroduced in 1953.

BODY COLOURS: DURATION OF USE (SERIES MM)

Colour	Introduced	Discontinued[1]
Platinum Grey	Sep 1948 (501)	Sep 1950 (63326)
Romain Green	Oct 1948 (510)	Sep 1950 (63489)
Black[2]	Oct 1948 (528)	—
Maroon	Dec 1948 (949)	Jun 1950 (49717)
Mist Green	Sep 1950 (63542)	Jun 1952 (151267)
Gascoyne Grey	Sep 1950 (63617)	Jul 1952 (153743)
Thames Blue	Sep 1950 (63706)	May 1952 (147638)
Clarendon Grey	Jun 1952 (149038)	—
Empire Green	Jul 1952 (151845)	—
Birch Grey	Jul 1952 (154129)	—
Maroon	Feb 1953 (177640)	—

[1]A dash denotes that the colour continued in use on 803cc Series II models.
[2]Black continued in use on saloons and convertibles until 1970.

PRODUCTION CHANGES

501 RHD
First Series MM two-door saloon built on 20 September 1948.

527 RHD
First Series MM tourer built on 14 October 1948.

904 RHD/5600 LHD (Dec 48)
Front suspension modified, fork to lower arm strengthened.

2117 RHD saloon (Jan 49)
3871 RHD tourer (Mar 49)
5856 RHD saloon (Jan 49)
6255 LHD tourer (Mar 49)
Last cars finished in cellulose paint.

5708 LHD (Jan 49)
First export car fitted with high-headlamp wings, marked USA in records.

3389 RHD/6142 LHD (Mar 49)
Flush-fitting circular rear light units incorporating stop lamps introduced. American models used pedestal type mounting.

Engine 3827 (Feb 49)
Modified speedometer drive assembly introduced with new oil seal and double hexagon.

16810 RHD (May 49)
Seat adjustment modified, carpet altered.

17580 RHD/7967 LHD (Jun 49)
Triangular profile helmet type rear stop tail light units fitted.

17840 RHD/8700 LHD (Jun 49)
Rear spring front mounting modified, renewable bush plates fitted.

18083 RHD/8888 LHD (Jun 49)
Sealing rubbers introduced for door window channels.

18885 RHD (Jul 49)
Door sealing rubbers changed: Sorbo replaced by moquette-covered clip-on type.

26102 RHD/10607 LHD (Oct 49)
Windscreen rubber channel, screen centre pillar and weather strip modified. Windscreen inner moulding discontinued.

27384 RHD/10006 LHD (Oct/Aug 49)
Bottom radiator hose arrangement changed: metal pipe and two-hose arrangement replaced by single bellows type hose.

29862 RHD/11958 LHD (Nov 49)
Steering modified, steering lever taper enlarged.

31782 RHD/12324 LHD (Dec 49)
Door surround/top painted instead of chromed.

31790 RHD/12338 LHD (Dec 49)
Front hub and stub shaft modified.

33241 RHD/12869 LHD (Dec 49)
Bonnet chain and fixing discontinued.

34490 RHD/13251 LHD (Jan 50)
Boot lock striker plate modified.

38471 RHD (Feb 50)
Fascia controls identified by letters on pull switches.

40835 RHD/43554 LHD (Mar/May 50)
Rear screen rubber and fittings changed. Inner moulding discontinued.

57681 RHD/54349 LHD (Jul 50)
Two sun visors fitted as standard to two-door saloons, available in grey and beige colours.

62551 RHD/65004 LHD (Sep 50)
Four-door saloon introduced. Specification included new high-headlamp wings. Separate side lights in revised grille panel, 7in headlamps. Stainless steel window surrounds, exterior chrome finisher on rear window rubber, exterior door handle escutcheons, one-piece bumper valance and blade front and rear, two wipers. Interior innovations included strap-type door pulls, interior light, armrests on rear doors, self-cancelling trafficators, demister ducts on fascia, ashtrays in front door panels.

63541 RHD/64813 LHD (Sep 50)
Maroon carpet and maroon piping for hood cover (tourer) discontinued.

63541 RHD/68068 LHD (Sep/Oct 50)
Wing piping in Maroon, Platinum Grey and Romain Green discontinued.

63542 RHD/65069 LHD (Sep 50)
Wing piping introduced in Thames Blue, Gascoyne Grey and Mist Green.

65736 LHD (Oct 50)
Oil filter fitted, oil pump and sump modified. Window ventilator assembly changed. New style catch fitted to two-door saloon and tourer (same as four-door saloon).

69622 RHD/71098 LHD (Oct 50)
Two-door saloon and tourer fitted with strap door pulls, each with a one-piece chrome-plated finisher.

69662 RHD/71222 LHD (Oct 50)
Petrol filler neck modified.

72985 RHD (Nov 50)
Increase to two wipers for home market on two-door saloon and tourer.

78235 RHD/73748 LHD (Dec 50)
Radiator top hose modified.

78593 RHD/73961 LHD (Dec 50)
Accelerator cable assembly modified.

Engine 77001 (Dec 50)
Changed to dynamo mounting bracket, exhaust manifold, carburettor and air silencer/cleaner. Impeller-type water pump fitted. Heater available as option on home-market models, but fitted as standard to North American models.

832024 RHD/81501 LHD (Jan 51)
Split bumper and fillet discontinued. One-piece valance and bumper blade introduced to two-door saloon.

83390 RHD/81595 LHD (Jan 51)
High-headlamp front wings along with new grille panel with side lights introduced for two-door saloon and tourer models. Chrome-plated grille insert retained.

90117 RHD/89726 LHD (Mar 51)
Painted radiator grille introduced. Chrome-plated grille available as an option March 1951. Painted hub caps with M motif later made available in black.

90318 RHD/89910 LHD (Mar 51)
Brake shoe assembly front and rear modified.

90685 RHD/93454 LHD (Apr 51)
Overriders fitted to bumper assembly on four-door saloon.

91982 RHD/99332 LHD (May 51)
Shock absorber pivot arm to upper link modified.

100920 RHD/102836 LHD (Jun 51)
Tourer redesignated convertible. Fixed rear side windows introduced for convertible models. Tourer detachable sidescreens discontinued. Hood sticks increased to five and tension wires fitted.

109699 RHD/110504 LHD (Aug 51)
Short bonnet discontinued. Re-designed bulkhead panel with full-size bonnet and extended drip moulding introduced for two-door saloon and convertible models. New style hinges and buffer to body side introduced August 1951.

114122 RHD/110707 LHD (Sep/Aug 51)
External rear screen chrome finisher discontinued on four-door saloon. Chrome hub caps reintroduced with M motif.

114502 RHD/110631 LHD (Sep/Aug 51)
Trafficator switch mounting bracket discontinued on four-door saloon.

114924 RHD/110813 LHD (Sep 51)
Front suspension top link modified.

123567 RHD/122232 LHD (Nov 51)
Convertible hood canopy changed, tension wires discontinued.

124810 RHD/122788 LHD (Dec 51)
Ashtray fitted to fascia grille on two-door saloon and tourer.

131461 RHD/126598 LHD (Jan 52)
Ashtrays discontinued in door panels on four-door saloon, introduced in fascia grille.

131858 RHD/126725 LHD (Jan 52)
Hub and brake drum modified.

139175 RHD/138415 LHD (Mar 52)
Headlamp beam warning light fitted on four-door saloon.

139360 RHD/139513 LHD (Mar 52)
Metal glove locker badge replaced by plastic one.

139439 RHD (Apr 52)
New type identification plate with F-type prefixes introduced on 1 April 1952: RHD and LHD car numbers no longer allocated in batches.

140823 (Apr 52)
Headlamp main beam warning light fitted on two-door saloon and convertible.

144454 RHD/144408 LHD (May 52)
Secondary steering rack damper fitted.

149078 (Jun 52)
Thames Blue wing piping discontinued.

149079 (Jun 52)
Clarendon Grey wing piping introduced. Steering column bracket support fitted.

151844 (Jul 52)
Birch Grey and Mist Green wing piping discontinued.

151845 (Jul 52)
Empire Green wing piping introduced.

159190 (Sep 52)
First CKD (Completely Knocked Down) vehicle with overhead valve engine.

160001 RHD (Aug 52)
Series MM sidevalve models and new Series II overhead valve models in production side by side.

170697 RHD (four-door saloon) (Dec 52)
174443 LHD (two-door saloon, convertible)
Flashing indicators fitted to North American cars.

176410 (Jan 53)
Final Series MM four-door saloon car number.

177640 (Feb 53)
Maroon wing piping re-introduced.

179820 (Feb 53)
Final Series MM convertible car number.

179839 (Feb 53)
Final Series MM two-door saloon car number.

MORRIS MINOR SERIES II (1952-56)

Continuity with the Series MM cars is illustrated well on this early Series II convertible, owned by Ian Murray and finished in Empire Green. From this angle, there is no change at all in body styling, trim or lighting.

One of the most significant developments in the British motor industry was the amalgamation in 1952 of the Austin Motor Company and the Nuffield Organisation, which included Morris Motors Limited, to form the British Motor Corporation (BMC). A direct consequence was the immediate availability of the 803cc overhead valve (ohv) engine used by Austin in the A30, its rival 'baby' saloon. This proved opportune for Morris and, not surprisingly, the new A-series engine was earmarked as a possible replacement for the ageing sidevalve unit which Morris had deployed as a stop-gap in 1948.

While Series MM production continued unabated until February 1953, ohv engines were being fitted simultaneously to selected four-door saloons destined for export from July 1952 – these ohv-powered cars were designated Series II models. With the eventual demise of the Series MM models, production of two-door saloons, convertibles and four-door saloons became exclusively Series II from 23 February 1953. In many respects the Series II cars remained the same as the Series MM, so much so that

at first the only external distinguishing feature was a new style bonnet motif and badge to replace the bonnet flash and badge used on the Series MMs.

The Series II model range was expanded twice in 1953. In May came the addition of van and pick-up commercial variants, and later in October the estate version – the Traveller – was announced.

All Series II models underwent a major facelift in October 1954. Significant changes to the internal and external body styling, as well as continuing updates of mechanical components, combined to make this a watershed in Series II production terms. As a result, Series II models are commonly referred to as 'early' and 'late.' For ease of reference, the descriptions which follow in this chapter will adopt this established distinction.

TRAVELLER

The emergence of the Morris Minor Traveller as an addition to the range followed development work on the larger Morris Oxford Series MO 'Traveller's Car' and its

launch into production in October 1952.

The Traveller was really a car of two halves. One half was based on the established front end assembly and floor pan of existing saloon and convertible models. The other half, a completely new arrangement, comprised an ash frame, aluminium side panels, an aluminium roof and a pair of ash-framed rear doors. These aluminium panels were used right through to the end of production in 1971. The ash frame, which was bolted to the front end assembly and the floor assembly, provided structural rigidity which was further enhanced by the inclusion of double-skinned inner box sections in the sills, a similar arrangement to that used on convertible models in order to compensate for the absence of the roof.

Four roof rails linked the cant rails and provided additional lateral support. The front rail was bolted to the inner steel flange of the cabin roof, while the rear top rail was jointed to the rear pillars and secured by a three-way metal plate fitted in the rear corners. Two centre rails provided additional support for the aluminium roof, which was fastened to the cant rail and rear top rail by

This late Series II two-door saloon belonging to Alan Prest is a 1955 model finished in Clarendon Grey. This grille style, with painted horizontal bars, replaced the original honeycomb design in October 1954, a year after the Series II was introduced.

The ash-framed 'Traveller's Car' – as it was billed – arrived with the launch of the Series II and proved to be a versatile vehicle, even if in this earliest form it was the heaviest Morris Minor ever produced. As on the four-door model, the trafficators are mounted high on the B post. For practical use on modern roads, this recently restored 1953 example – owned by Bryan Gostling and believed to be the oldest surviving Traveller – is fitted with a rear fog lamp, indicators, reflectors, a reversing lamp and a tow bar.

1in galvanised nails. A drip moulding, also fastened by nails, served as an outer finisher. Two sliding windows were located between runners placed in the cant rails and middle rails on either side of the car.

One-piece steel wings designed specifically for use on the Traveller were screwed to the underside of the jointed wheelarch panels. In keeping with other models, matching coloured wing piping was fitted. Three other significant differences in the metal body structure on the Traveller distinguish it from other models: the B posts are wider and incorporate caged nuts for locating the ash frame at its forward end, the boot floor assembly lacks the curved structure of the saloons, and the inner wheelarch panels have a different profile.

The ash frame fitted to the very early Series II vehicles differed slightly in certain respects from that of later models. In particular the bottom panel linking the front pillar and the wheelarch panel changed. The early type flush fitting wooden inner panels were superseded by 'footers' which overlapped the outer edge of the adjoining panels.

Anyone contemplating restoring or

Each of the rear door pillars on the Traveller has a single aperture for a flat-profile stop/tail lamp. Hinges are painted body colour and no badging is included on the rear doors. The circular reflector and the auxiliary lamps partially concealed by the bumper are owner-added extras.

The design of this part of the ash frame on the Series II Traveller was changed for later models: here the 'footer' fits flush to each of the adjoining panels.

Catches on the side windows of Series II Travellers were chrome-plated. Seen here with the window open, the catch operated with a swivel action to secure the window in a closed position.

replacing ash sections on the early Travellers would be well advised to enlist the help of a good specialist. Although 'off-the-shelf' replacement parts are available for later Minor 1000 models and many are interchangeable with the Series II, some are unique to the early cars. Having one-off sections made to original specification is often the only answer – as in the case of the rear pillars which have a single aperture for a rear light. Later versions have two holes and are clearly not appropriate if originality is to be maintained.

BODY & CHASSIS

So far as the saloon and convertible models are concerned, there were no significant changes to the body structure or styling when the Series II was introduced. This was due, in part, to the fact that the late Series MM models had been produced alongside the new Series IIs and there had been a lengthy transition period. During this time the profile of the bulkhead had been altered to allow clearance for the overhead valve engine. Consequently, there was no real difference in the monocoque construction or external body panels of the late Series MMs and the early Series IIs.

However, the major update in October 1954 changed all that. As well as a redesigned fascia panel accommodating a centrally placed speedometer, there was a significant external evolution with the decision to change the front grille design. The 'cheesegrater' grille, as this feature of the early Morris Minors is affectionately known, was replaced by a slatted grille with horizontal bars. At the same time, the front wings were altered to accommodate repositioned sidelight units, which were previously in the grille panel. This development had significant repercussions for the construction of the front wings. In manufacturing terms, it meant that a third element had to be added to the previous two-piece pressing in order to accommodate the new grille panel and the sidelight fittings.

Other knock-on effects included the redesign of the front valance, which was re-shaped to accommodate the new contours created by the revision of the wings and grille panel, and the redesign of the chrome 'hockey sticks', which served to fasten the front edges of the wings to the grille panel.

BODY TRIM

The clean flowing lines of the later Series MM models carried through to the early

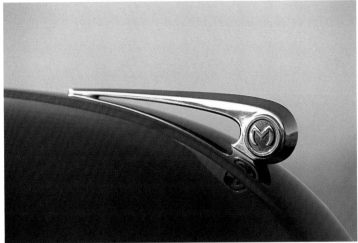

A new style of Mazak bonnet flash with a separate M motif on each side (above) and an enlarged Mazak bonnet badge (left) are the only external features which distinguished early Series IIs from previous models.

The importance of the Series II's October 1954 update is clear in these two comparative photographs (above). The sidelights were repositioned on to the wings, the grille changed to a horizontal bar design, the profile of the front wings altered, the headlamp surround adjustment was deleted, the profile of the 'hockey stick' altered and a chromed inner grille surround was introduced. In addition, a revised front bumper valance was required because of the changed profile of the grille panel.

Series II vehicles with few significant changes. Notable exceptions were the new style bonnet flash and the enlarged bonnet badge. These items of brightwork assumed increased significance on the early Series II cars because they were the only external features which distinguished them from the Series MMs.

The bonnet flash is an interesting feature for a number of reasons. Its appearance belies the fact that the M motifs which appear on either side of the Mazak casting are separate items – listed as 'medallions' in the parts list. Good quality original items are much sought after, given that on subsequent models a revised one-piece casting was adopted. A further point of interest is that in some countries the profile of the bonnet flash was deemed to be dangerous and it was later banned on safety grounds. As a consequence, cars supplied to Scandinavian countries, for example, reverted to using the flush-fitting bonnet flash and badge used on the Series MMs.

Following the update of the front grille, an additional item of trim was introduced, an inner grille surround being fitted to the

later Series II models. Initially it was available as a chrome-plated item, but later an alloy version was produced. The chrome-plated type became part of the specification for Deluxe models in much the same way as overriders did. In all other respects the chromed parts fitted to the Series II saloons and convertibles remained unchanged.

The use of body-coloured wing piping continued on both front and rear wings on all models until car chassis number 307869 and Traveller chassis number 305719, when it ceased to be fitted to the front wings.

Chromework on the Traveller followed the pattern for all other models except that the rear bumpers were unique. Additional items of brightwork on the Traveller included plated side window catches and a locking rear door handle.

The Series II's split screen arrangement is exactly the same as that used on late Series MMs.

Although the small rear screen, special body moulding and rear badging remained unchanged on all Series IIs, the rear lights were different on later models.

This revised rear lamp unit introduced in October 1954 as part of the Series II update has a plastic cover incorporating a reflector. It was a marked improvement on the smaller glass triangular lamp which it replaced. Note also the continued use of body-coloured piping on the rear wings.

LIGHTING

The lighting arrangement on early Series II saloon and convertible models remained the same as it had been on the last of the Series MMs, but the introduction of the Traveller added another dimension to the rear lights. Rear stop/tail lights were fitted either side of the car in an aperture located towards the base of each of the rear pillars. The moulded glass had a fairly flat profile and was secured in the rubber mounting by a chrome bezel. Later models had an additional reflector mounted either side just above the light unit so as to comply with the 1954 lighting regulations.

The 7in F700 pre-focus bulb-type head-lamps continued to be used for all models, the only notable change being the phasing out of the split-type chrome surround, with its external securing screw mechanism, in

favour of a simpler one-piece chrome surround at car number 170679. Separate sidelights continued in use after the grille was altered and the sidelights moved to the front wings.

Rear lights on saloon and convertible models changed in 1954. Prior to this the triangular 'helmet' lamps first used on the Series MM were fitted. Stricter legislation on the use of reflectors forced a slight modification to these units, and preceded the introduction of a new style of lamp for the Series II saloons and convertibles. For the interim arrangement, externally mounted reflectors were fixed to brackets which were located between the lamp base and the lamp glass, and secured in the normal way by chrome screws and a retaining chrome bezel. This stop-gap measure satisfied the legal requirements while a rethink on the rear lamp design was applied.

The outcome was a larger rear lamp with an integral reflector in the lamp lens. The metal base of the unit was painted body colour while the rim which surrounded the bulb holder was chrome-plated. The plastic lamp lens was secured by two chrome-plated screws.

Number plate lamps remained unchanged on saloon and convertible models, but it should be noted that on Traveller models two lamps were used, one at each side of the number plate. Black metal covers with a single chrome-plated hexagon screw were standard specification for these lamp units.

It is worth noting that more stringent MoT requirements can lead to difficulties being encountered with lighting requirements on these pre-1954 cars. It is generally accepted that the single badge-mounted reflector is, by itself, inadequate for today's safety standards. The factory solution

This view of an original hood, fitted on this car from new, shows the small celluloid rear screen which was retained until the end of Series II production.

A useful interior shot showing the winged bolt which fastens the front rail to the screen surround. Contrary to expectations, this original item is not chromed.

For those owners replacing or restoring a Series II hood, the detailed stitching shown on this original hood will be a useful reference. The finisher on the front edge is nailed to the wooden front rail.

described above in relation to reflectors is a useful strategy which can be employed today without compromising original specification. Too often rear wings and bumpers are unnecessarily altered to accommodate the addition of reflectors for safety and MoT reasons.

WEATHER EQUIPMENT

The hood arrangement on the Series II models was a little different from the earlier Series MM type. Beige was the only colour offered from the beginning of production until late 1956, when two additional colours, green and red, were a welcome addition which significantly enhanced the character of the open cars. Matching coloured front rails added to the overall effect, as did the use of maroon and green

The mounting bracket for the hood frame is unobtrusive, which is more than can be said for the hood frame itself, shown here in its original gold colour (left). The rear seat and side panel on this 22,000-mile convertible are original and unblemished.

The full extent of the October 1954 update of the interior for the later Series II is evident here in the revised fascia panel, central speedometer and open gloveboxes. The seats, carpet and door trims on this car are original.

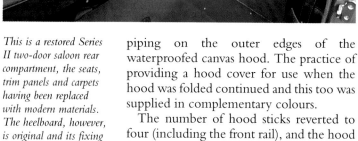

This is a restored Series II two-door saloon rear compartment, the seats, trim panels and carpets having been replaced with modern materials. The heelboard, however, is original and its fixing screws are clearly seen. Seat belts are an owner-added safety feature.

piping on the outer edges of the waterproofed canvas hood. The practice of providing a hood cover for use when the hood was folded continued and this too was supplied in complementary colours.

The number of hood sticks reverted to four (including the front rail), and the hood frame was painted the same gold colour as the steering column, the front edge of the parcel shelf and the heater – when one was fitted! In all other respects the hood fixings remained unchanged. The shape and dimensions of the celluloid rear window panel remained the same as the Series MM convertibles, with all the attendant difficulties for rearward visibility.

INTERIOR TRIM

The transition from Series MM to Series II had virtually no effect on the interior trim of saloon and convertible models. The same materials and patterns were adopted for seating and trim panels in the early Series II cars, with maroon and green being the dominant colours for door sealing rubber coverings, upholstery and carpets. Matching seat and trim piping continued to be used.

However, the introduction of a differently shaped gearbox cover panel, along with a repositioned gear lever, did force changes in the shape and cut of the front carpet for all Series II models. This revision was accompanied by a change to the rear carpet, which reverted to a one-piece mat covering the transmission tunnel and floor. Four matching carpet pads were sewn on to the rear carpet in an attempt to combat the excessive wear caused by the front seat frames resting on the floor. This change was also an attempt to treat a more serious problem, but it was in vain because many floor pans now show

With the passenger seat removed, the Series II Traveller's rubber floor mat – this is an extremely rare original item which came to light as part of a job lot at an autojumble! – can be seen clearly. Other Traveller features to note include the black-painted heel board and the carpeted wheelarches, the latter being a feature of Deluxe versions only. The sills were normally left body colour on both Standard and Deluxe models.

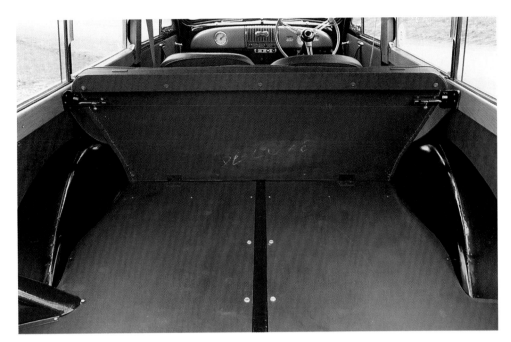

With the rear seat folded, the full extent of the loading capacity can be seen. The seat base was simply pulled forward using one or both of the 'pulls' shown. Locating plates fastened to the top edge of the back seat and the seat base hold them firm when in the folded position.

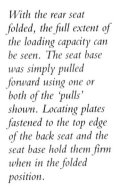

evidence of metal fatigue at these points, particularly if there has been a succession of owners of ample proportions!

Other improvements included more extensive use of underfelt. The front inner wheelarch cover pieces were supplemented by two full-size, specially-shaped front and rear pieces. The use of Veltex fastenings continued, as did the inclusion of a rubber heel pad on the driver's side of the front carpet. A further modification to the front carpet occurred in August 1956 when the gearbox cover panel was modified once again and the pedals were realigned to create more space between them. In addition the rear ashtray on four-door saloons was altered from its position across the transmission tunnel to one where it was placed lengthways on top of it.

The introduction of Deluxe and Standard specifications in 1953 had an impact on the interior trim options available to buyers. This was most noticeable in the cabin of the Traveller, which in standard form was fitted with a one-piece black moulded rubber mat covering the floor area but leaving the inner sills and the front inner wheelarches as exposed body colour. On very early Travellers, the loading area immediately behind the rear seat was also left exposed. Two specially-shaped black wooden boards made up the rear platform immediately above the spare wheel compartment. The rear inner wheelarches and rear side panels were left uncovered and were painted body colour. Standard models had Vynide seat and trim panels.

Deluxe Travellers retained the black rubber floor covering, but an additional feature was the use of carpet to cover the front inner wheelarch panels. Other Deluxe specifications for Travellers included a

The spare wheel compartment on the Traveller mirrors that of the saloons, remaining 'open' on the Series II Traveller.

The use of a Rexine-covered board headlining was discontinued on saloons in October 1954 in favour of this one-piece beige fabric headlining. A single sun visor was standard issue.

covered loading area with a rubber mat secured by aluminium wearing strips, and leather seating with Vynide trim panels.

On saloon and convertible models, carpets were fitted as standard. Deluxe specification on these models included leather upholstery and an extra sun visor.

A significant change to the seating in the Series II range preceded the major facelift in October 1954. Although the front seats retained their basic shape, the backrests and bases were modified. The previous interlocking spring arrangement was replaced by a solid seat base, easily identified by its black colour and regular pattern of holes.

The backrests on the early type of Series MM style front seats had Vynide-covered fibreboard backings 'invisibly' tacked to the seat frame. However, some time after the new style coverings were introduced, a different method of assembly was adopted, coinciding with the introduction of seat covers with integral sewn backings for the seat back. During assembly the seat covers were placed over the back of the seat frame and the backing boards were inserted into the 'envelope' created. This method of assembly became established practice during 1954, but there was a transition period during which both methods were used with the new style facings. As a consequence, owners faced with the restoration or refurbishment of front seats need to check carefully on the construction of the seats before ordering replacement trimming kits.

The later Series II seat facings were significantly different in appearance. Instead of the horizontal panels of the Series MM

type, much narrower vertical fluted panels were introduced. On the driver and passenger seats, five narrow panels were incorporated into the seat cushion and backrest. On rear seats, the pattern was repeated twice on both the seat cushion and backrest. The profile of the fluting was quite pronounced due to the fact that the seat padding was more substantial. This type continued until the end of production and persisted even when the seat frames were altered again for two-door saloon, convertible and Traveller models to create fixed-back front seats. In spite of having less padding, the earlier seats are thought by many to be more comfortable.

Vynide trim remained unchanged, with plain door panels and specially shaped rear side panels incorporating an integral armrest on two-door saloon, convertible and Traveller models. Four-door saloons continued to have a dual-purpose armrest and door pull fitted to the rear doors, and a chrome-plated trim strip attached to both front and rear door panels. New replacement finishers are not available, so it is important that the originals are retained for use on refurbished or replacement panels.

For a time, early Series IIs retained the Rexine-covered three-piece board headlining used on the later Series MM saloons. Traveller models had a similar three-piece arrangement for the front cabin, supplemented by a one-piece board for the rear roof section. The Rexine covering continued to be available in beige or light grey.

The board headlining was discontinued late in 1953 on saloon models in favour of

a one-piece light grey or dark beige fabric headlining. This was supported by four rods and tensioned by wires which ran the length of the outer edges and which were secured at either end and at the B posts. Traveller models, however, retained the earlier board headlinings throughout production of the Series II.

DASHBOARD & INSTRUMENTS

Early Series II cars – including for a short time the newly-announced Traveller – retained all the features of the late Series MM dashboard, but the major change to a new fascia pressing in October 1954 led to the introduction of a central speedometer with open gloveboxes to either side. The open gloveboxes significantly altered the appearance of the fascia, and in the opinion of many people made it look more spartan.

In general terms, all instrumentation can be said to have been compressed into the 5in speedometer which incorporated odometer, fuel gauge and warning lights. More specifically, the speedometer, type AJA 5063 with a bronze face and black lettering, was calibrated to record speeds in excess of 80mph. Numbers on the odometer were white on black. Of the four warning lights – red for ignition, orange for oil pressure, red for headlamp main beam and green for indicators – only three were operative on home-market models, for the indicator light was used solely on Series II LHD export models which were fitted with flashing indicators. RHD models were fitted with trafficators and the warning light did not operate when these were in use.

The control switches operated as before and were little changed in appearance. They retained their brown colouring and white lettering. A symmetrical appearance was achieved for the control switches with the inclusion of the wiper switch alongside the choke, lights and starter controls – previously it had been positioned centrally on top of the dashboard. The self-cancelling type of trafficator switch used on four-door models was also adopted on Travellers, while the brown non-cancelling type with integral warning light continued in use on two-door saloon and convertible models.

A fascia panel illumination control switch similar in design to the one fitted to models with the early dashboard was incorporated into the new fascia. It was conveniently placed centrally on the underside of the fascia panel – although in truth some owners probably never realised it was there and many others rarely used it!

When fitted, the Smiths recirculatory heater was centrally positioned beneath the fascia panel and above the parcel tray. The outer metal casing was painted gold to match the leading edge of the parcel tray and the steering column. The brown control switch, which determined the variable speed of the heater fan, had white lettering in keeping with other control switches. This heater was standard on Deluxe models, optional on home market Standard models, and standard on export Standard models except those destined for hot climates.

An additional change with the later dashboard arrangement was the position of the ashtray. Previously it had been unobtrusively placed in the centre of the fascia grille panel. There was no room for an ashtray on the new style fascia with open gloveboxes either side of the central speedometer, so it was added, almost as an afterthought, to the underside of the fascia panel just beneath the passenger glove compartment.

ENGINE

The overhead valve engine used to power the Series II Morris Minors originated with the Austin Motor Company. Since this engine had already proved to be successful in the Austin A30 (launched as the Austin Seven in 1951), the timely merger between Austin and Morris provided an opportunity for the redoubtable A series unit to show its worth in the heavier Morris Minor. This was

This informative shot, taken prior to the completion of the restoration of this 1953 convertible, hence the absence of a parcel shelf, illustrates again the similarity between the late Series MMs and the early Series IIs. The same dashboard and instruments, seats, door and trim panels are used. The absence of a parcel shelf allows a good view of the Smiths recirculatory heater, the pedal rubbers with their ribbed pattern, and the revised cut of the carpet to suit the new gear lever position and the reshaped gearbox cover panel. The locating pins for the front rail of the hood can also be seen. The chromed finisher cap for the door sealing rubber should be painted body colour.

The later dashboard, introduced at the October 1954 update, shows the central speedometer, new switch positions, open gloveboxes and dash-mounted ashtray. The speedometer, interestingly, is correct in having an additional warning light for indicators, even though these were not fitted on home market models.

no mean task given that this 803cc engine was the smallest fitted to any British car at that time.

Contemporary road-testers were full of praise for the new engine and enthused about the increased acceleration and tractability it brought to the Minor. Here are some of the salient observations. *The Motor*: 'Improved performance results from use of an 803cc overhead valve engine with 7.2:1 compression ratio in place of a 918cc sidevalve unit with 6.6:1 compression ratio...'

The Autocar: 'The overhead valve engine has a smaller swept volume than the sidevalve unit but it is capable of revving faster and delivers an ultimate maximum 30bhp at 4800rpm as against 27.5bhp for the sidevalve... Performance tests show that the maximum speed is little changed, the latest car showing an improvement of 1mph, but there is considerable improvement in acceleration times. For example, acceleration from 10-30mph in top gear takes just over 16secs as compared with 23.5secs with the

The 803cc overhead valve engine as fitted to the Series II range, seen here with the oil bath air filter which was an export option. This car is fitted with a heater. The high-domed radiator is a characteristic feature of the Series II models. The battery tray liner has been personalised and the wooden side rails should be painted black.

sidevalve engine. At the same time there is, however, a slight drop in the maximum speeds obtainable on the gears; the maximum normally used in third is now 34mph with an ultimate 42mph, whereas with the sidevalve the figures were 38mph and 46mph respectively.'

The Autocar also observed that the new engine was lighter than its predecessor, and expressed confidence that acceleration in top gear would impress anyone who had driven the equivalent sidevalve model. Cynical observers, of course, would reply that anything would be an improvement on the top-gear acceleration of a sidevalve Minor – even a Series II!

The new engine was designated APHM and when fitted to the Morris Minor the cast-iron block, cylinder head and pressed steel rocker cover were painted green. Exceptions to this did occur, as light blue coloured engines were also occasionally fitted as standard specification to Series IIs – no particular significance attaches to this alternative choice of colour. Engine ancillaries such as the dynamo and starter motor were also generally painted green or blue to match the rest of the engine, but variations do exist as the Lucas Service parts were, and still are, supplied with the yoke of the components painted black. Consequently, there is a 'grey' area in terms of originality concerning 'factory finish' or

original supplier's specification.

The four-cylinder engine has a bore of 57.9mm and a stroke of 76.2mm. The valves, set in line in the cylinder head, are operated by rockers and pushrods from the camshaft in the left-hand side of the cylinder block. Oil seals are fitted to the valves and there is the normal provision on the rockers for clearance adjustment. The camshaft is driven by roller chain from the crankshaft and has twin chain adjusters. At the timing gear end, the camshaft has a steel-backed white metal bearing, while the other two bearings are direct in the crankcase. The oil pump and distributor are driven from the camshaft, the latter by a transverse shaft with a helical gear drive.

The split-skirt pistons are constructed of aluminium alloy with an anodized finish, and carry three compression rings and a slotted oil control ring. The gudgeon pins are clamped in the connecting rods, which have steel-backed white metal renewable big-end bearings. Three steel-backed white metal renewable bearings support the forged-steel counterbalanced crankshaft, the thrust being taken by the centre main bearing.

Oil supply is carried in the steel sump below the cylinder block and the oil filler cap is fitted to the valve rocker cover. The dipstick, marked to show maximum and minimum levels, is situated on the right-

hand side of the engine (as viewed from the driving position), while the oil pump, an eccentric vane type, is mounted on the rear end of the crankcase. A unique feature of the Series II engine is the throwaway type bypass oil filter carried on the right-hand side of the crankcase and connected to the main oil gallery by a drilled passage. Earlier cars have an oil pipe connecting the oil pressure gauge and the rear end of the main gallery. Later Series II cars have an oil pressure switch fitted to the rear end of the main gallery in order to control the oil pressure warning light on the central speedometer dial.

COOLING SYSTEM

A new and more efficient cooling system was employed with the 803cc overhead valve engine. In the opinion of many it was long overdue, so the demise of the series MM's thermosyphon system was not lamented for long. A significant difference was the reduction in capacity from 13½ pints to 9¼ pints and the introduction of a slimmer radiator with a much smaller header tank, easily distinguished by its domed profile.

Water was circulated within the pressurised sealed system by a vane type water pump mounted at the front of the engine. This water pump is unique to Series II models and not interchangeable with later

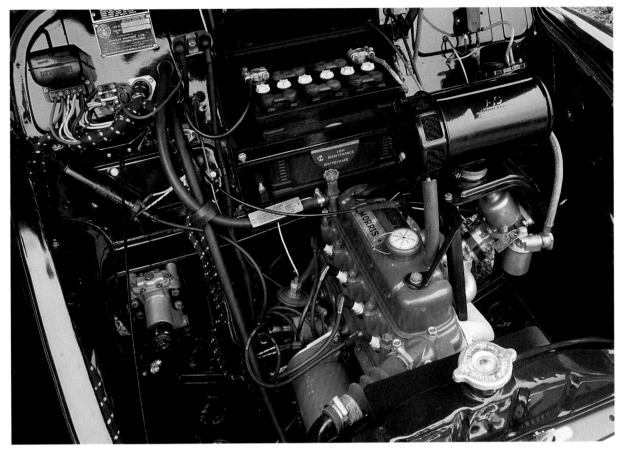

A home market version of the 803cc engine, showing the distinctive gauze air cleaner assembly. The only obvious departure from originality is that jubilee clips have been used in preference to adjustable wire clips on the radiator hoses.

versions. Cooling was assisted by air being drawn through the radiator by a fan attached to the water pump pulley. To enable the system to be drained, drain taps were fitted to the base of the radiator and at the rear of the engine block adjacent to the exhaust manifold.

Changes occurred in the type of hoses used during Series II production. Fabric-covered moulded rubber hoses were phased out and replaced by plain moulded rubber hoses secured by adjustable wire clips.

FUEL SYSTEM

All the major Series MM fuel system components continued in use on the A-series engine of the Series II, the only significant development relating to the carburettor. The H1 type 1⅛in SU carburettor continued to be used but in a slightly different guise, as a 30° semi-downdraught version. The inclined mounting of this type of carburettor assisted the delivery of the fuel mixture to the combustion chambers.

Other developments included a revised fuel filler arrangement for the new Traveller model – a specially-moulded rubber support mounting was fitted to the aluminium side panel for the filler pipe – and the use of a new gauze air cleaner assembly on home-market models. With its distinctive cylindrical shape and tall mounting brackets, all

painted black, this air cleaner dominated the engine bay and remains a unique feature of Series II models. Export models continued to be fitted with a black-painted oil-bath air cleaner, but the version fitted to Series II models differed slightly from the earlier MM type in that the cover and filter element assembly were one-piece instead of separate components.

EXHAUST SYSTEM

The original type of exhaust fitted to the Series II models was available as a one-piece unit, comprising a front downpipe, silencer and tailpipe. At the front end it was secured to the manifold by a split-collar clamp, fastened by two bolts and nuts. Two metal support brackets similar to those used on the earlier Series MM cars used 'Balata' belting, a slightly flexible material, to support the tail pipe. A feature of the original silencer was the provision of drain holes along the bottom seam to allow condensed moisture to be blown out by exhaust gas pressure.

The separate aluminium inlet and cast-iron exhaust manifolds used with the 803cc overhead valve engine were mounted on studs and secured to the cylinder head by six brass nuts and four large washers. A special joint sandwiched between the manifolds provided a hot spot, allowing heat from the exhaust to warm the ingoing fuel mixture.

The exhaust manifold was painted matt black, while the inlet manifold was left in its natural aluminium finish.

ELECTRICS

With the exception of the following changes to components used, the electrical system remained unaltered for Series II models.

The Lucas battery was changed to type GTW7 A/2, the distributor to type DM2 (service number 40299) and the Champion spark plugs became type NA-8. The dynamo (Lucas C39PV/2) and starter motor (Lucas M35G/1) remained unchanged.

The black-painted Q12 coil (service number 45020) used on the early Series II models was the same as on Series MM cars, and was mounted on the bulkhead panel close to the inner wing. This version was superseded in April 1955 by type LA12 – with a natural alloy finish – when a mounting on the dynamo was adopted.

TRANSMISSION

The clutch assembly, which utilised the Borg & Beck 6¼in disc-type single-plate clutch, remained unchanged except for a slight amendment to the adjustment mechanism. Used this time in conjunction with a different four-speed gearbox, it operated just as efficiently as before.

The 803cc gearbox, characterised by its straight gear lever, had a number of unique features. Top gear was obtained by direct drive, second and third gears were in constant mesh, while first and reverse were obtained by sliding spur gears. As with the sidevalve gearbox, synchromesh was available on second, third and fourth gears. Engagement of reverse gear involved moving the gear lever to the extreme right of the neutral position and lifting it upwards, before moving it still further to the right and bringing it backwards to engage the gear.

The gearbox ratios were the subject of much debate and some criticism that they were ill-chosen. The ratios are: first, 4.09:1; second, 2.588:1; third, 1.679:1; top, 1.000:1; reverse, 5.174:1.

Hardy Spicer type universal joints and propshaft were used as before, although the sliding joint arrangement was altered to accommodate 'fore and aft' axle movement. A sliding joint of the reverse spline type was fitted between the gearbox and the front universal joint flange. Lubrication was provided by oil from the gearbox and consequently the previous use of a grease nipple at this point was dispensed with. The previous practice of painting the propshaft black continued, although the gearbox outer casing retained its metal finish.

The same rear axle fitted to the Series MM models was used initially on the early Series II saloon and convertible. The semi-floating axle, characterised by its split casing, was eventually superseded by a new, one-piece, three-quarter floating axle which had the differential carrier assembly bolted into the front. First fitted to the Traveller, it became part of the standard specification for all models in January 1954, and, like the earlier axle, it was painted black.

In the effort to update the Series II and improve acceleration, the rear axle ratio changed too, the earlier MM ratio of 4.55:1 being displaced by a lower ratio of 5.375:1.

Apart from the obvious variation in construction, the main difference between the two axles is that on the semi-floating type the halfshafts are not only subject to torque but also to shear stresses because the axle supports the hub and brake drum. On the three-quarter floating axle, the halfshafts are only subjected to torque. In spite of contemporary exhortations to fit complete replacement units where possible, more repair and maintenance work can be carried out with this axle *in situ* than was previously possible.

This is an original 5.00-14 crossply tyre, but highlighted here in non-original style as if to emphasise that these tyres are rarely seen nowadays – 5.20-14 tyres are usually fitted. The three-pin fixing for locating the hub cap continued in use from the Series MM, but the hole in the wheel for brake adjustment was deleted.

SUSPENSION

'If it ain't broke don't fix it' is an adage which could well be applied to the design of the suspension on the Morris Minor. Justifiable praise was heaped on the car's designers from the outset and much was made of the success of the suspension layout, so it is not surprising that few modifications were made.

Developments for Series II models included a modified swivel pin assembly introduced early in production at car number 161856. This modification, which could be applied retrospectively to all cars, included a new swivel pin lower link which was fitted with a bush, thrust washer and a sealing ring. A further improvement related to the shock absorbers and occurred in January 1954, when the DAS8 Armstrong units (front) were replaced by type DAS8/R. These later dampers have a special seal fitted to the rebound piston to prevent high temperature fade, and were originally distinguished from the earlier type by the addition of a spot of green paint. The rear shock absorbers have the same modification, but are more easily distinguished from the earlier type by thicker flanges which require the use of longer mounting bolts, and by the valve being horizontal below the bump piston.

STEERING

Rack and pinion steering proved its worth in the Morris Minor Series MM and so not surprisingly it remained virtually unchanged for Series II models. Small-scale improvements to the outer ball sockets included improved seals and the addition of grease nipples.

The 16in steering wheel with its central horn push continued to be used even after the fascia was significantly updated in the later Series II cars. In keeping with earlier models, the steering column and steering wheel centre boss were still painted gold.

BRAKES

All the established features of the hydraulic braking system of the Series MM cars continued in use on Series II models. Provision for an improved method of brake adjustment via an aperture in the road wheel, first used on later Series MMs, was carried forward to Series IIs fitted with wheels which had the pin-type fixing. It was not an option, however, on the later wheels which used moulded contours to retain the hub caps.

No significant changes occurred on the early Series IIs fitted with the MM type axle, but the switch to the BMC A-type rear axle prompted changes in the brake assembly. Separate brake drum and hub assemblies were introduced and the front wheel cylinders were modified. New Lockheed part numbers 35000 (front right) and 35001 (front left) replaced the MM front cylinders, although the rear cylinders remained unchanged (34577).

WHEELS & TYRES

The wheels and tyres of the Series MMs continued to be fitted to the early Series II saloon and convertibles, but the introduction of the new rear axle – first to the Traveller in October 1953 and to the rest of the range in January 1954 – necessitated the production of a completely new wheel pressing. The overall wheel size remained at 14in but the spacing between the centre holes differed significantly, rendering interchangeability with Series MMs and earlier

Series II models impossible.

Initially the three-pin fixing arrangement for the hub caps continued on these new wheels, although the positioning changed to accommodate new and larger hub caps, which were chrome-plated and embossed with the M motif in keeping with previous practice. Like the earlier Series MM wheels, these revised Series II wheels were prone to cracking, particularly around the stud holes, so a stronger wheel was eventually produced for Series II models. These later wheels are distinguished by their integral moulded pressings which serve to locate the hub caps, and the provision on the rim for fitting the new style valve used in conjunction with tubeless tyres. A consequence of this development is that owners of Series IIs fitted with the A-type rear axle have a choice of wheels, even though the earlier cars were fitted with the pin-type fixing wheels originally.

The tyres were still 5.00–14 Dunlops and recommended pressures remained at 22lb sq/in (unladen) or 24lb sq/in (laden).

The arrangement for stowing and securing the spare wheel remained unchanged, and was adopted for the Traveller. The easy access to the spare was the subject of favourable comments from road testers, who felt that a separate boot compartment (cars) and loading area (Travellers) was a 'real boon'.

TOOL KIT

The tool kit issued with Series II models was slightly altered and contained the following items: distributor screwdriver and gauge, tyre pump, tyre valve spanner, screw type jack, combined wheel brace and hub cap remover, Tecalemit grease gun, screwdriver, box spanner, three open-ended spanners, 9in tommy bar, starting handle and tyre lever. On later models fitted with the new rear axle, a key was supplied for removing and replacing the drain plug on the rear axle. The open tool roll supplied in two colours, black or brown, had two matching cloth ties attached.

EXPORT VARIATIONS

For Series II models, the same Series MM export specifications continued to apply, although it is interesting to note the following advice contained in a BMC salesman's handbook for 1953: 'The heater will not be fitted on Deluxe cars for delivery to

A redesigned chassis plate which reflected the 1952 change in identification code was fitted to all Series II vehicles.

overseas territories where it is not applicable (hot climates). Overriders and heaters are available as extra to standard specification for delivery to overseas. Cars to North America will either be to Standard or Deluxe specification but with equipment peculiar to the American market: flashing indicators, laminated windshields, induction heaters and twin horns.' In addition, the dipswitch mechanism on left-hand drive North American models was mounted on a special bracket in a more conventional floor-mounted position adjacent to the inner wheelarch.

Exterior trim remained largely unchanged for export models, except that safety legislation in Switzerland led to a decision to retain the Series MM bonnet flash and badge instead of using the new badging of the Series II models. Similar legislation was introduced in Denmark on 1 January 1957 (shortly after the start of Minor 1000 production), and also required that all older Series II cars had their bonnet motifs removed.

An additional feature on left-hand drive Series II models was a different pedal arrangement necessitated by modifications to the gearbox cover resulting from the use of a separate master cylinder cover plate. The right-hand drive brake pedal replaced the existing left-hand drive pedal, the clutch pedal pad was repositioned to the left-hand side of the clutch lever, and a modified accelerator pedal was introduced.

Whereas home market Series II models used Lucas 354 (dip left) 42/36W double-filament bulbs in the 7in headlamp units, North American cars used Lucas 301 (dip right) 36/36W bulbs and European cars (except France) used Lucas 360 (dip vertical) 45/35W bulbs.

SERIES II PRODUCTION FIGURES

	Total
1952	2422
1953	53942
1954	72837
1955	88058
1956	52579
Total	**269838**

Note
A production breakdown for the individual body styles is not possible for the Series II.

IDENTIFICATION, DATING & PRODUCTION

The later style of identification plate introduced in April 1952 continued in use for all Series II models. The only additional feature was the adoption of the model identification code L for the Traveller model. For example, FLA 11 would be a home market Traveller finished in black synthetic paint.

Unlike the Series MM engine, which had a circular brass engine number plate attached to the side of the block, the overhead valve engine had a small rectangular identification plate attached to the top of the block in a position where it was much easier to read.

The main run of car numbers for Series II models is 180001 to 448714, but the following lower brackets of numbers were also Series II: 159190 to 159201; 160001 to 161021; 170001 to 171000; 178501 to 179800. The prefix for Series II engines is APHM.

Towards the end of Series II production in 1956, there are a few Minor 1000 cars with 948cc engines in the bracket 448042 to 448714. Again, these vehicles are easily distinguished because they have very low engine numbers of three or four figures, whereas Series II models produced by this time had six-figure engine numbers.

OPTIONAL EXTRAS & ACCESSORIES

A modest increase in the range of optional extras occurred during Series II production. On Standard and Deluxe models an HMV radio could be specified as an extra, while for Standard models only it was possible to specify leather seating and a heater. Late in production a fresh air heater kit became available.

Accessories available during the period 1952-56 included the following:

Wing mirrors
Travel rug
External sun visor (metal)
Headlamp peaks
Lucas fog lamp
Chrome-plated badge bar
Radiator blind
Locking petrol cap
Windscreen washer (kit)

COLOUR SCHEMES (SERIES II MODELS)

Paint	Trim	Carpets
Jul 1952 to Oct 1954 (saloon/convertible)		
Black	Maroon	Maroon
Clarendon Grey	Maroon	Maroon
Empire Green	Green	Green
Birch Grey	Maroon	Maroon
Oct 1953 to Oct 1954 (Traveller)		
Black	Maroon	Black[1]
Clarendon Grey	Maroon	Black[1]
Empire Green	Green	Black[1]
Birch Grey	Maroon	Black[1]
Oct 1954 to Oct 1955 (all models[2])		
Black	Maroon	Maroon
Empire Green	Green	Green
Clarendon Grey	Maroon	Maroon
Smoke Blue[3]	Maroon	Maroon
Sandy Beige	Maroon	Maroon
Oct 1955 to Sep 1956 (saloon/convertible)		
Black	Maroon	Maroon
Clarendon Grey	Maroon	Maroon
Empire Green	Green	Green
Sandy Beige	Maroon	Maroon
Sage Green[4]	Green	Green
Dark Green[4]	Grey	Green
Birch Grey[5]	Maroon	Maroon
Oct 1955 to Sep 1956 (Traveller)		
Black	Maroon	Black[6]
Clarendon Grey	Maroon	Black[6]
Empire Green	Green	Black[6]
Sandy Beige	Maroon	Black[6]

[1]Black rubber floor mats were fitted to Standard Traveller models, but on Deluxe models maroon or green carpets covered the front wheelarch panels.
[2]Travellers were available in all these colours but continued to be fitted with black rubber mats instead of carpets, with the exception of the wheelarch covers on Deluxe models.
[3]Smoke Blue was replaced by Sandy Beige in February 1955.
[4]Sage Green and Dark Green were introduced in May 1956.
[5]Birch Grey was re-introduced in May 1956.
[6]Travellers in standard form continued to have black rubber floor mats to the end of Series II production.

BODY COLOUR: DURATION OF USE (SERIES II MODELS)

Colour	Introduced[1]	Discontinued[1]	Notes
Maroon	–	Feb 1953 (184201)	Used on approx 400 cars
Black	–	–	Used throughout
Clarendon Grey	–	–	Used throughout
Empire Green	–	Apr 1956 (426894)	Saloon/convertible
	–	Sep 1956 (448714)	Traveller
Birch Grey	–	Oct 1954 (289575)	
	May 1956 (430282)	–	Resumed use for saloon/convertible
Smoke Blue	Oct 1954 (290385)	Feb 1955 (316731)	Saloon/convertible
	Oct 1954 (289798)	Feb 1955 (313418)	Traveller
Sandy Beige	Feb 1955 (319579)	May 1956 (433334)	Saloon/convertible
	Feb 1955 (313543)	Sep 1956 (448560)	Traveller
Dark Green	May 1956 (430352)	–	Saloon/convertible
Sage Green	May 1956 (427459)	–	Saloon/convertible

[1]A dash denotes that the colour continued in use from Series MM models and/or onwards to 948cc Minor 1000 models.

PRODUCTION CHANGES

CHANGES BY CAR NUMBER

160001 (Aug 52)
First overhead valve engine fitted in four-door saloon.

180001 (Feb 53)
All models fitted with OHV engine.

182745 (Feb 53)
Crown wheel bolts increased to ⅜in diameter.

184760 (Mar 53)
Wheel bolts with larger hexagon, 0.705in/0.710in, introduced.

198690 (Jun 53)
Rubber boots introduced on steering joints, ⁵⁄₁₆in diameter clutch rod fitted.

205839 (Jul 53)
Suppressors fitted on ignition wiring.

205850 (Jul 53)
Larger glass channels and rubbers introduced to improve seal on front quarterlights.

210866 (Aug 53)
Exhaust system modified.

216901 (Oct 53)
Traveller introduced, Standard and Deluxe specification choices available.

220001 (Oct 53)
One-piece fabric type roof lining introduced for saloons.

221803 (four-door saloon) (Oct 53)
221842 (two-door saloon)
221914 (convertible)
Deluxe models introduced featuring heater, leather seats, overriders and passenger sun visor.

228267 (Dec 53)
A-type rear axle introduced. Standard swivel pin assembly fitted. Wheels modified: wheel studs and nuts replace bolt fixing.

228766 (Traveller) (Nov/Dec 53)
228510 (four-door)
232055 (two-door, convertible)
New front seat frames fitted with revised Vynide and leather patterns.

240671 (Feb 54)
Improved shock absorbers fitted.

264013 (Jun 54)
Engine steady cable fitted to gearbox mounting bracket.

283545 (Sep 54)
Separate reflectors fitted to Traveller.

284948 (Sep 54)
Rear reflectors mounted on a bracket on rear light units for saloons and convertibles.

289687 (Traveller) (Oct 54)
290173 (four-door)
291140 (two-door)
291336 (convertible)
Horizontal grille bars introduced. Revised instrument and control panel. Central speedometer with integral fuel gauge introduced with open glove boxes each side.

293051 (Dec 54)
New larger rear light fitting incorporating reflectors on the lens cover.

295948 (Traveller) (Nov 54)
299097 (car)
Engine steady fixing to bulkhead introduced to reduce clutch judder.

305719 (Traveller) (Jan 55)
307869 (car)
Wing piping discontinued on front wings.

329069 (Traveller) (May 55)
338930 (two-door, convertible)
338932 (four-door)
Wiring loom modified to take account of the revised position of coil, now fitted on top of dynamo.

357172 (Traveller) (May 55)
361959 (car)
Grease nipples fitted to handbrake cables.

419860 (Traveller) (May 56)
433613 (car)
Position of foot pedals changed; gearbox cover and master cylinder cover panel modified to provide more footroom.

433571 (May 56)
Green and red convertible hoods added to the range.

440238 (Jun 56)
Front seat frames modified on two-door saloon and convertible models, now fixed back instead of folding.

448714 (Sep 56)
Series II production discontinued.

CHANGES BY ENGINE AND GEARBOX NUMBER

693 (engine) (Sep 52)
Modified oil pump drive.

926 (engine) (Oct 52)
Introduction of modified carburettor and manifold distance-piece, gudgeon pin clamping screw with larger head. Oil release valve spring modified to give lower pressure.

1859 (engine) (Nov 52)
Chamfered compression ring introduced in second ring groove.

4025 (engine) (Jan 53)
Timing arrow and timing mark on pulley introduced.

12684 (engine) (Mar 53)
Improved water pump pulley.

29644 (engine) (Jul 53)
New flywheel starter ring mounting.

6363 (gearbox)
Gearbox rear dust cover discontinued.

45023 (engine) (Oct 53)
Introduction of distributor with high-lift cam.

56578 (engine) (Dec 53)
Spark plug gap altered to 0.20in – 0.22in.

58088 (engine) (Dec 53)
Speedometer cable with ¾in × 26 TPI at gearbox introduced.

61601 (engine) (Jan 54)
Dustproof carburettor introduced.

9176 (gearbox)
Modified first and second speed synchromesh fitted.

72610 (engine) (Feb 54)
'Super Seal' introduced in water pump, different profile fan belt fitted on revised pulley wheels.

83161 (engine) (Apr 54)
Modified clutch drive plate.

83314 (engine) (Apr 54)
Burman oil pump introduced as alternative to Hobourn-Eaton.

88347 (engine) (Apr 54)
New locking plates for rocker shaft.

93798 (engine) (Apr 54)
Modified flywheel dowels.

MORRIS MINOR 1000 (1956-62)

The first of the Morris Minor 1000 models, with a single-pane windscreen and enlarged rear window. Owned by Ian Millington, this 1957 four-door saloon displays the contrasting grey wheels and grille bars which were the standard colour for black cars.

A sense of *déjà vu* prevailed at the London Motor Show at Earls Court in 1956 when the new Morris Minor 1000 stole the limelight. Memories of 1948 were evoked as an expectant public had their first glimpse of the restyled Morris Minor. The up to date styling of its new bodyshell and the car's potential for increased performance, provided by an improved gearbox and a more powerful engine, excited contemporary road-testers. Their enthusiastic scribblings later confirmed that the Morris Minor had 'come of age', and that here indeed was a car to be reckoned with. For many people today, the Minor 1000 of this era epitomises all that is good about the Minor.

windscreen and a new style inner windscreen surround, forming a new roof panel which was 'transplanted' on to the established lower body structure. Coupled with new one-piece front and rear curved screens, the effect was considerable. The safety advantages of better visibility were further enhanced by the continued use of Triplex safety glass. All these amendments to the saloons were replicated where appropriate on convertible and Traveller models.

An additional new feature was the changed profile of the rear wings. Although they were fitted in exactly the same way as before, their fuller shape (with a smaller wheelarch cutout) served to conceal more of the inner wheelarch.

BODY & CHASSIS

The underframe and front end assembly of the monocoque body remained unchanged on the new model, but the decision to dispense with the split windscreen (in order to improve forward visibility) and to enlarge the rear screen resulted in a comprehensive revision of the upper body structure and the fascia panel.

In the case of saloon models, this meant much narrower front screen pillars, an enlarged rear screen aperture, a changed profile to the top and bottom edges of the

BODY TRIM

The revised styling of the Minor 1000 facelifted the overall appearance, but in terms of external body trim and chromework there was little change, the only significant difference from previous models relating to badging.

The earlier Morris Minor badges on the bonnet and boot lid of saloon and convertible models were replaced by Minor 1000 ones. On Travellers, the same arrangement applied except that the rear badge was fastened on the right-hand rear door. A

chromed effect was retained on the windscreen rubber with the introduction of a new two-piece finisher inserted into the outer edge of the windscreen rubber – a throwback to the split-windscreen days. Two additional outer finishers positioned in the middle of the top and bottom edges concealed the joints.

All other items – bonnet and boot hinges, bonnet motif and badge, boot handle, door handles and escutcheons, hub caps, bumpers, hockey sticks, top grille bar and the inner grille surround – remained unchanged. Deluxe specification continued to include overriders, while four-door saloons and Travellers were fitted with stainless steel door window surrounds.

LIGHTING

Lighting components were carried forward from the Series II to the Minor 1000, and initially the only significant change involved the rear light unit fitted to saloon and convertible models. Instead of the earlier chrome bezel fitted on to a body-colour lamp base, a larger chrome bezel now fitted flush to the rear wing.

Trafficators continued in use on all models, although it has to be said that their usefulness was being questioned by the late 1950s. Flashing indicators, of course, had been part of the specification for export models bound for North America since the early 1950s, but it was not until October 1961 that the trafficators were eventually discontinued and the 'American system' of flashing indicators became standard on all home-market Morris Minors.

In effect, the new indicators were operated through the existing front sidelights and rear brake lights. With the assistance of a relay box and flasher unit, the indicators were activated by a self-cancelling stalk on the

Vastly improved rearward visibility was provided by the wraparound rear screen, while rear wings with a fuller appearance were a new feature as well. This later two-door saloon dating from 1961 and owned by Barry Tibbetts shows that few external changes occurred during 948cc production, but the use of Old English White for wheels, grille and coachline on this Clipper Blue example was one of many changes in colour scheme evolution.

Larger, stronger wipers with a revised fixing for the blades operated with a 'clap hands' action on the toughened single-pane screen.

The facility to fold down the rear seat back (below) to provide additional storage space was a standard feature on all Morris Minor saloons.

The boot compartment changed little on the Minor 1000 models, but an additional feature, just visible here, is the position of the fastener which holds the rear seat back in place.

steering column. When the indicators were in use, the brake light on the other side of the car would still function in the normal way.

Consequences of this changed arrangement included the fitting of a nickel-plated relay unit with screw fittings, a flasher unit with an alloy body in the engine bay on the inner flitch panel, and the enlargement of the front sidelight glasses to accommodate the larger twin filament bulb which was fitted.

This was a far from satisfactory system which prompted many owners to make modifications in an effort to be safer on the road. It is still a contentious area today with MoT testers, many of whom do not accept the absence of an amber indicator even though the system was the original specification for 948cc Minor 1000 models after October 1961.

Separate headlamps and sidelights (left) continued in use on the 948cc Minor 1000, and the design of the front wing, grille panel, bumper and front valance remained unchanged from their introduction in 1954 as part of the Series II update.

This 1961 model was one of the last to be fitted with trafficators. Blanking panels were fitted for a time after they were discontinued in favour of flashing indicators.

WEATHER EQUIPMENT

Amendments on convertible models to the design of the hood reflected the all-round improvement in visibility on the saloons. A much larger rectangular plastic rear window prompted a road-tester on *The Motor* to observe that 'a truly transparent rear window of quite large size provides good vision'.

The use of a canvas hood continued up to September 1957, when a plastic covered material was introduced. As well as providing added protection from the elements, this change broadened the scope for introducing new colours (see 'Colour Schemes' later in this chapter). The only criticism of the hood arrangement recorded by *The Motor* in 1959 concerned the time taken to stow the hood: 'If the design has a limitation, it is that with a dozen press-stud hood fixings above and behind the windows as well as the usual two fastenings above the windscreen, and six press-studs on the neat hood bag, weatherproofness has been combined with complete folding of the roof by acceptance of the need for single-handed raising or folding away to take several minutes'.

INTERIOR TRIM

One of the distinctive features of the 948cc Minor 1000 range is the wide variety of seat and trim combinations offered in the 1956-62 period. No doubt contemporary sales personnel were happy with the ever-extending choice of colour combinations and trim options, but for the modern day owner and restorer ensuring that the original specification is retained can, at first, seem a daunting prospect. There were three distinctive types of interior.

The first style featured from the start of production in 1956 and carried through to early 1959. Available in the three colours of Maroon (also known as 'Morris Red'), Dark Sage Green and Grey, it followed closely the pattern adopted in the later Series II interior. Although it featured the established five fluted panels, replicated twice on the rear seats, the general appearance was changed due to the fact that the seat backrests and cushions had a much flatter profile. An additional feature, which had been included on some of the last Series II cars, was the extensive use of contrasting piping on the outer edges of the seat backrests and cushions as well as on the plain door panels and side panels of two-door saloons, convertibles and Travellers. It is alleged that this use of contrasting piping was due to the influence of the Austin arm of the BMC partnership. However, caution needs to be exercised as its use did not extend throughout the whole of the time this type of interior was fitted, so owners who find that their seats are fitted with matching piping should not panic!

The seat frames remained unchanged except that the earlier solid seat base on two-door saloons, Travellers and convertibles was replaced by a rubber seat webbing attached to the frame by metal clips. Four-door Standard and Deluxe models continued with the solid seat base until car number 579359, at which point the new arrangement was adopted and the folding driver's seat was changed to a fixed back type.

Another feature of the first type of interior was the use of matching trim material for the padded roll on the front edge of the parcel shelf, a concession to safety added to the specification for the new Minor 1000. Maroon was used up to number 693331, Dark Sage Green to 693807 and Grey to 693588.

A Minor 1000 badge replaced the earlier winged casting with its integral reflector. The rear lamp unit on Minor 1000 models has a larger flush-fitting chrome bezel and the boot handle no longer has an external screw fitting.

Two views of a 1960 948cc convertible, showing the larger rear screen (left, above) introduced for the hoods on these models and the left-hand drive layout of a North American export version (left, below). This Pearl Grey car, owned from new by Rear Admiral Joseph F. Quilter, is unusual in having matching Pearl Grey wheels and grille, while the faded hood was originally maroon. The sticker on the front grille panel is a US Navy identification plate.

The second type of interior used between 1959-61 featured a new style of seating with broad panels on both the seat backrest and cushions. Colours available were the familiar red and green, and the two new colours of Oxford Beige and Blue-grey. On the front seats four vertical panels were complemented by a single horizontal panel on the top of the backrest and on the leading edge of the cushion. Rear seats had a similar arrangement except that the seven inner vertical panels were flanked on either side by a single contoured vertical panel. Plain leathercloth door and side panels in matching colours were fitted to all models, although leather seat facings were reserved for Deluxe versions.

At the time this revised interior was introduced, the parcel shelf was enlarged to accommodate a revised heater arrangement which included a long overdue refinement – the fitting of a shroud to conceal the main body of the unit. The choice of pearl grey as the colour for this shroud provided continuity with the headlining and the front edge of the parcel shelf. Interestingly, the steering column now passed through the parcel shelf.

The third style of interior, often referred to as the duo-tone type, was available from 1961, and became a transitional feature as this design continued in use after 948cc production ceased. Restricted to Deluxe models, duo-tone upholstery was available in the following combinations: Tartan Red/Silver Beige, Porcelain Green/Silver Beige and Blue-grey/Silver Beige. The introduction of this new Deluxe interior also ended the use of leather upholstery on Deluxe models.

The seat covers reverted to a fluted style with eight vertical panels topped by a horizontal panel on the backrest and a specially padded horizontal panel on the leading edge of the cushion. Rear seats had 15 vertical panels in similar style. Door panels were also duo-tone, with a contrasting Silver Beige centre panel sandwiched between two main colour panels. The same basic pattern was replicated for Standard models but only in single colours of Tartan Red, Porcelain Green or Blue-grey. With this style of interior the parcel shelf roll, heater shroud and headlining were finished in light beige.

Carpets in the 948cc range changed, mainly as a result of the larger gearbox cover panel and remote control gear lever. For all models fitted with carpets, the front floor area now consisted of separate driver and passenger sections and a two-piece gearbox and transmission tunnel cover. An additional feature was the inclusion of a rubber pad adjacent to the clutch pedal. In all other respects the carpet set remained unchanged.

Provision was still made for fitting rubber mats to Standard version Travellers. A revised one-piece moulded rubber mat specially designed for 948cc vehicles was available for use throughout production. An improved two-piece plastic-coated covering was also produced for the rear loading area and the back of the rear seat squab of the Traveller. Held in place by aluminium wearing strips, this durable cover also provided effective sound deadening. The Rexine board type headlining continued in use for a time on Traveller models, but in April 1957 a two-piece fitted headlining was adopted in the same type of material used on other models.

The useful facility for folding down the rear seat squab was retained on all models. However, the 'lift the dot' arrangement which was first use in 1948 was superseded on saloons and convertibles in 1961 by a winged bolt fastened through the metal rear seat squab support. Prior to this, the 'lift the dot' arrangement, which had originally been located inside the car, was moved to the boot area at car number 497597 early in 948cc production.

DASHBOARD & INSTRUMENTS

A return to the use of glovebox lids significantly altered the appearance of the fascia on the new Minor 1000. Painted body

Contrasting grey piping was a feature of the first style of interior, fitted to Minor 1000 models between 1956-59. The front seat frames on this 1957 model are very similar to late Series II ones.

An unusual photograph of a Clipper Blue Traveller (below), showing the rear seat back folded forward with the seat base in place. Interesting features include the lidded gloveboxes, swivelling window catches, and the trimmed seat back with aluminium wearing strips.

While the seats in this 1958 four-door model (left) follow the earliest Minor 1000 material and pattern, their frames have been modified and give the seat backrest and base a squarer appearance.

The interior trim changes were adopted on all models. Here the Blue-grey broad-panelled style – the second of the three trim patterns found on 948cc models – is seen in original form in a Traveller (below), along with matching plain trim panels.

Broad panels on the seat upholstery characterise the second style of interior, fitted to the Minor 1000 between 1959-61, this being the Blue-grey variation.

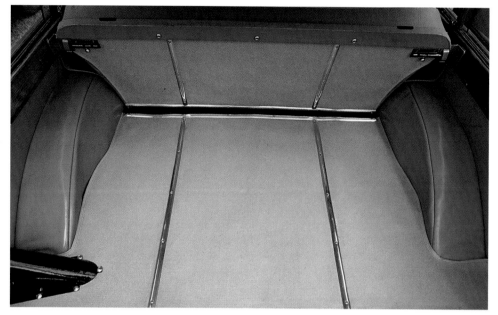

Compared with the spartan load space of Series II Travellers, covered wheelarches, side trim panels and a rear floor covering add significantly to the overall appearance of this 1961 model.

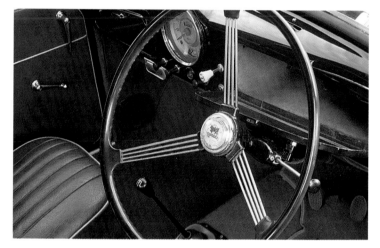

Headlining fabric colours –variously Light Grey, Pearl Grey and Light Beige – changed frequently on Minor 1000 models.

colour to match the rest of the fascia, the lids were fitted to both driver and passenger sides. Some people queried the usefulness of the driver's side compartment as access was severely restricted by the obstruction of the opening lid and the steering wheel. An alternative use of the space recommended by the manufacturer was to fit a loudspeaker in conjunction with the optional radio.

The central speedometer remained unchanged in general appearance from the late Series II type, but it was calibrated differently to take account of the changed axle ratio. Details of the range of speedometers fitted to 948cc models and their identification codes are listed in the accompanying table. Unlike the earlier Series II arrangement, however, all four warning lights were operative on all models in the Minor 1000 range. The indicator operating light – previously defunct on home market models – was now illuminated

when the trafficators were activated by the new style of steering column indicator stalk, which doubled as a horn control as the previous centre horn push on the steering wheel had been displaced by a colourful Morris emblem. The control switch layout continued as before, but the switches themselves were now coloured black with clues to their function designated in white lettering. In the interests of continuity, the Smiths recirculatory heater now sported a black outer casing and the rheostat control switch was marked in a similar fashion to all the other switches.

The combined indicator/horn push stalk was roundly criticised. The arrangement did not find favour with *The Autocar*'s road tester: 'The trafficator operating arm is combined in one unit with the horn button below the steering wheel on the right-hand side. It is non self-cancelling and as the trafficator arms are housed in the central door pillar (four-

Many customers questioned the wisdom of having a glovebox lid on the driver's side – one can see why. This type of dished 'safety' steering wheel arrived with the 948cc model. The much-improved position of the gear lever can also be seen, its proximity to the driver – coupled with an improved gearbox – making gearchanges effortless. The loudspeaker on the inner wheelarch trim panel is a later addition.

On Deluxe versions, the duo-tone pattern extended to door trim panels – and to all four doors on those models. In contrast to this two-door saloon, the B post casing above the waistline on four-door cars was Silver Beige, but below the waistline it was finished in the main trim colour.

As with earlier Morris Minors, the 948cc models retained a folding/tipping arrangement for the passenger seat to allow easy access to the rear. An interesting feature of late 948cc cars fitted with this style of interior is the return to open gloveboxes.

Duo-tone upholstery, introduced in 1961, was the third interior style fitted to the 948cc Minor 1000 models, but its use was reserved for Deluxe models. This is an original example of the Silver Beige/ Porcelain Green combination. On standard models this fluting pattern on the seats was retained, but without Silver Beige inserts.

SPEEDOMETER IDENTIFICATION (948cc MODELS, MPH)

Identification	Final drive	Model	Chassis numbers
SN4401/9	5.375:1	2dr/4dr/conv	448801-579227
		Trav	448801-572906
SN4406/08	5.375:1	2dr/4dr/conv	579228-990289
SN4477/10		Trav	572907-990289
		Disabled	558301-925075
SN4401/15	4.555:1	2dr/4dr/conv	448801-579227
SN4451/15		Trav	448801-572906
SN4466/00	4.555:1	2dr/4dr/conv	579228-953663
SN4407/00		Trav	572907-953663
SN4477/00	4.555:1	2dr/4dr/conv	953664-990289
		Disabled	957001 onwards

door), the driver cannot see them in daylight. Although a green 'indicator in operation' signal is incorporated into the single circular all-purpose instrument, it does not give adequate indication. Combination of the horn with the trafficator arm has demanded a heavy pressure for operation to avoid inadvertent dual action and thus in both the functions which this unit has to perform it has shortcomings.'

Strong words! A year later, when a Traveller version was tested, the protests continued in spite of attempts to improve things: 'Semaphore indicators are non self-cancelling – a constant source of annoyance, in spite of a warning lamp on the quadrant of the steering column lever. This lamp is provided with a hinged shield to reduce brightness at night. The button for the powerful horn is on the end of this lever

which can lead to inadvertent signalling.' The mention of the new indicator warning lamp is informative: previously located in the speedometer, it moved to a quadrant at the base of the column stalk in October 1957, intermittently from car number 549923 and on all vehicles from 555415.

The problem was eventually solved at car number 705622 in March 1959 when a steering column mounted self-cancelling direction indicator switch was adopted and the horn push returned to the centre of the steering wheel. This revision led to the use of a new style horn push with a gold 'M' motif on a red background and to a change in the speedometer, which now had three warning lights instead of four – the indicator warning light being surplus to requirements because there was now a green light on the end of the stalk. At this point the main beam

This Deluxe interior shows two changes which arrived with the broad-panelled upholstery style in 1959: the parcel shelf is larger and the Smiths recirculatory heater is now concealed behind a Pearl Grey shroud.

Early cars had stark, plain metal glovebox lids, but in late 1959 this more refined appearance (below), with inner liners secured by a plated metal surround, was introduced. An additional support bracket was installed because the lid is heavier. Glovebox lids disappeared again in 1961.

The central motif on the Minor 1000 steering wheel is purely decorative, as the horn push is now on the end of the trafficator stalk, an arrangement which generated strong press and customer criticism at the time. The horn push returned to the steering wheel in March 1959, when a new indicator stalk with a green light at its end also arrived.

warning light also changed from red to blue.

During the remaining period of 948cc production, amendments to the fascia revolved around the glovebox lids. In late 1959 they were upgraded with the addition of a liner held in a place by a polished metal finisher, but in 1961 they were discontinued – so once again the Morris Minor had open gloveboxes. Other features, including the under-fascia ashtray and the ubiquitous (and elusive) fascia panel illumination switch, remained constant.

The speedometer of 948cc cars retains the four warning lights of the Series II version and the control switches remain the same. The use of glovebox lids, however, tells us that this dashboard belongs to a Minor 1000. The white switch is a period fitting for the Tudor windscreen washer.

ENGINE

The 948cc engine was an instant success mainly due to the extra power provided by increased cubic capacity. Combined with a far superior gearbox (with closer ratios) and an altered back axle ratio (raised to suit the performance increase), it enhanced the

The 948cc A-series engine on early models was dominated by an imposing AC oil bath air filter. Many rebuilt engines, of which this is one, are painted in various 'mix-and-match' shades of green because the original colour specification is no longer available. By common consensus, the closest modern match is Land Rover Mid Bronze Green.

reputation of the Morris Minor yet again and contributed in no small measure to a sharp upturn in sales.

Although similar in general construction to the first overhead valve engine fitted to the Series II Minor, the 948cc version was different in many detail respects. *The Autocar* put these changes into perspective succinctly in its 1957 road test with the following description: 'The third, present stage of this successful model is designated the Minor 1000, which indicates the nominal capacity of the engine. The actual capacity is 948cc, an increase of 145cc over its predecessor. It is achieved by enlarging the cylinder bore from 58mm to 62.9mm, but this is not done by merely boring out the previous cylinder block; there is now a new casting which has been strengthened to accommodate the higher power involved. In this category of modification are larger diameter big end bearings and strengthened connecting rods; these changes have also helped to stiffen the crankshaft.'

The Morris tradition of extensive road testing of prototype models continued after the merger with Austin to form BMC. Prototypes of the Minor 1000 were extensively tested in Europe, and high-speed tests in which the cars averaged over 60mph for 25,000 miles led to significant changes in the final specification of the engine in production form. Testing proved that white metal main and big end bearings exhibited evidence of fatigue while comparable lead-bronze bearings were unmarked after sustained high-speed usage. In spite of the additional cost involved, the stronger bearings were fitted to production models. Consequently, the connecting rods have steel-backed, lead-bronze, lead-indium (or copper-lead, lead-tin) plated surface renewable bearings.

Additional features of the 948cc engine include the fact that the split-skirt pistons are of aluminium alloy with an 'alumilited' finish, and that cylinders 1/2 and 3/4 do not have a water passage between them. A further change to the earlier 803cc version was the adoption of a full-flow oil filter with a renewable element instead of the previous external throwaway type. Like the 803cc engine, the block and rocker cover of the 948cc engine were painted green, and a Morris label was applied to the rocker cover.

COOLING SYSTEM

The principal features of the cooling system adopted on the Series II overhead valve engine were retained. An improved water pump, not interchangeable with the earlier type, was fitted to the 948cc block. The Series II type radiator, distinguished by its domed header tank, continued in use until 1960, when it was replaced by a different version with a flatter top to the header tank. The drain tap arrangement on both block and radiator remained unchanged.

The only other features worthy of note relate to the provision of a fresh air heater. This was an option on early 948cc vehicles and an additional kit was available to enable a conversion to be made. From car number 654750, a blanking plate was fitted to the floor panel beneath the parcel shelf for the fresh air intake. Secured by screws, this could easily be removed if the decision was taken to proceed with the conversion. The components in the kit enabled air ducting to be fitted around the existing recirculatory heater unit, provision to be made for a fresh air intake and for improvements to the efficiency of the water circulation in the heater system. Towards the end of 948cc production, this fresh air heater was incorporated into the heater assembly on Deluxe models.

FUEL SYSTEM

From 1957, it was possible to travel further on a tank of petrol as the capacity was increased from a paltry five gallons to a respectable six and a half, a long overdue development which had been called for years

This 948cc engine fitted to a later car has the Cooper paper air cleaner assembly — dubbed the 'saucepan' type. Also clearly visible is the engine steady bar which attaches the engine block to the bulkhead.

earlier in the motoring press. The SU type L fuel pump, which had been used on all Minors since 1948, continued to provide sterling service, but changed slightly during 948cc production when the union on the pump linking it to the carburettor changed from a threaded pattern to a push-on fit with a securing clip.

The 1¼in SU H2 carburettor used on the new model was larger than the type H1 used on the Series II, but otherwise many of its features were the same. However, it was subject to a number of slight modifications, the most noticeable being the switch from brass to steel levers for the choke and accelerator linkage. In 1960, the H2 carburettor was replaced by the HS2, which is easily distinguished by an improved design of flexible steel-braided nylon feed pipe running from the bottom of the float chamber to the jet, the nylon pipe being moulded into the jet and dispensing with the need for sealing glands at top and bottom. Further amendments to the accelerator cable throttle return spring, mixture control and vacuum advance control pipe improved the general functioning of the carburettor, but operation and adjustment remained the same in principle as previous types.

Every new type of engine fitted to the Morris Minor was accompanied by a redesigned air cleaner assembly. The new style of oil bath cleaner fitted from the beginning of Minor 1000 production was of equally imposing proportions as the gauze type fitted to the 803cc engine. Finished in black, this AC unit was fitted for a limited period only, being replaced by a smaller and more dignified Cooper-type paper air cleaner in February 1959. Commonly referred to as the 'saucepan type' and still painted black, its proportions were much more in keeping with the cubic capacity of a vehicle which the advertising department at BMC chose to highlight as 'the biggest small car buy'.

Late in 948cc production, a modified air cleaner assembly became available as a service item. This version's breather pipe was altered to run from the rocker cover to the air intake pipe (the 'saucepan handle') of the filter, whereas previously the breather pipe had run from the rocker cover to the elbow on which the filter unit was mounted. As a consequence, late 948cc vehicles may be fitted with either type of air cleaner.

EXHAUST SYSTEM

The mild steel exhaust system fitted to the 948cc Minor 1000 models was the same as that used on the Series II vehicles. The split collar arrangement used to locate the front pipe to the manifold and the other mounting brackets remained unchanged, as did the underfloor asbestos heat shield. As with previous models, the manifold was finished in matt black. The only significant development involved the exhaust and inlet manifolds: on early cars, up to September 1959, these were separate units, but an integral unit was substituted after this date.

ELECTRICS

The already established positive earth 12 volt electrical system continued in use on the new Minor 1000. The use of certain Lucas components also continued, in particular the dynamo-mounted model LA12 coil, model M35G starter motor, model C39 PV-2 dynamo and model RB106-2 voltage control box. An updated Lucas 12 volt model GT 7E Lucas battery was fitted as standard, while spark plugs were changed to Champion N5.

A new distributor, model DM2 P4, was used on 948cc models almost to the end of production, but it was replaced at engine number 604228 in 1962 by a new type, 25D4. Identification of the different types is simple as the model number is visible on the casting adjacent to the vacuum advance unit, and the shapes of the distributor bodies are noticeably different.

Two types of wiper motor were used, both being fitted in a new exposed position in the engine bay. An improvement on the earlier mounting under the fascia, this new position allowed much easier access for maintenance. Lucas model DR2 was replaced by model DR3A in November 1961 at car number 939695, the DR3A keeping the 100° angle of wipe introduced on later versions of the DR2; on the 1000's introduction in 1956, the angle of wipe had been 110°. The 'clap hands' wiper action continued in use.

The main body or yoke on engine ancillaries such as the dynamo and starter was painted in the same green as the engine. The coil retained its alloy finish, while the distributor cap and the cover on the voltage regulator were brown. The single Windtone horn fitted to home market models was originally mounted on the tie plate in the bottom of the engine bay and painted black, but for Minor 1000s it was repositioned on a special bracket on the radiator cowling.

TRANSMISSION

The 6¼in Borg & Beck dry clutch assembly continued in service, this time in

Single Windtone horns were fitted to home market models. This type is correct for a 1961 car.

conjunction with a revised gearbox which featured a new remote control gear change and improved ratios. The main outer casing was the same as before, but the rear extension casing was modified to house the remote control mechanism.

This refinement, which greatly enhanced the smoothness of the gear change, was the subject of a great deal of favourable comment. In 1958, *The Autocar* tested a Minor 1000 Traveller and observed: 'Smoothness through the speed range and instant response to throttle openings are well liked qualities of the 948cc engine. The engine of the Traveller was no exception and the gear change, which must be among the best on any car made today, was a pleasure to use.'

Gear selection was certainly much improved and the use of reverse gear was greatly simplified in comparison with the previous Series II arrangement. Improvements in overall performance were due in no small measure to improved gear ratios. *The Autocar* again: 'It would have been impossible to take advantage of the improved engine characteristics if the overall gear ratios had not been altered also. Higher gearing in the axle (4.55 ratio superseding the previous 5.375) has raised the mean maximum speed by a little over 8mph. But, more important, the new gearbox ratios have vastly improved the performance on the intermediate gears. Maximum speed in third is increased from 42mph to 59mph, and a proportionate advantage is achieved in second gear.'

The new gear ratios were: first, 3.628:1; second, 2.374:1; third, 1.412:1; fourth, 1.000:1; reverse, 4.664:1. Synchromesh still operated on second, third and top gears.

The propeller shaft, rear axle casing, universal joints and front sliding joint remained the same as they had been on the

Series II. The only significant change was in the choice of crown wheel and pinion utilised in order to change the axle ratio from 5.375:1 to 4.55:1. The external finish of all components remained unchanged, with a cast finish for the gearbox and black paint on the back axle and propshaft.

SUSPENSION

Apart from two changes which occurred early in 948cc Minor 1000 production, the suspension layout and its constituent parts remained unchanged. The updates comprised stronger swivel pin assemblies and a rearrangement to the rear spring assembly. On saloons and convertibles, the number of rear spring leaves was reduced from seven to five and the thickness of each leaf was increased from ⅞in to ¼in. The heavier Traveller models retained the seven-leaf arrangement.

STEERING

The rack and pinion steering system fitted to the Minor 1000 continued largely as before, except for a change to the steering column assembly and the addition of improved oil seals on the rack. Details of the combined horn and indicator switch, the problems associated with it and subsequent updates have been covered in the 'Dashboard & Instruments' section.

The later steering column assembly with the central horn push is interchangeable with the earlier type, so a swop may have occurred over the years. Some vehicles may also have been fitted with a period accessory which enabled a second stalk to be fitted to the steering column to operate the horn independently of the combined indicator/horn stalk. Clearly this is an area

Unlike most Series II models, Minor 1000 wheels have a contoured moulding which serves to locate the hub cap.

where modifications may have occurred and where attention to detail is important if originality is sought – albeit at a sacrifice to convenience in this instance.

A new type of 'safety' steering wheel was introduced for the Minor 1000. Coloured black and sporting a colourful Morris emblem in the centre boss, this dished wheel had three spokes, each comprising four chromed wires. From March 1959, a centre horn push replaced the coloured motif, but all other features remained unchanged. The steering column was now painted black.

BRAKES

The hydraulic braking system used on the Minor 1000 remained the same as it had been at the end of Series II production. Most components are interchangeable on model types manufactured between 1954-62. The only major change was the handbrake lever, which on the new 948cc cars was much more compact and used a chrome-plated push-button release mechanism on the end of the lever itself; previously the release mechanism had been on the top edge of the lever. The handbrake lever was painted black.

WHEELS & TYRES

Pressed steel disc road wheels were used on the Minor 1000. Like the final type of wheel fitted to the Series II, contoured mouldings were used to secure the hub caps and no provision was made to allow brake adjustment with the wheel in place. Dunlop C41 5.00-14 crossply tyres were fitted and chrome hub caps were used.

On introduction, wheels were finished in body colour for all models except those painted black, turquoise or dark green, which featured Birch Grey wheels. On black cars the horizontal grille bars were also painted grey. This was the beginning of a trend which became firmly established – from February 1959 almost all models had contrasting road wheels and grille bars. At first these were finished in an off-white colour - Pearl Grey – but after July 1960 Old English White was used. The exceptions to the rule were Old English White and Pearl Grey vehicles, whose grilles and wheels matched the body colour.

TOOL KIT

The size of the tool kit supplied with 948cc Morris 1000 models varied during production. Up to car number 848240, the following items were supplied in a canvas tool roll: starting handle/wheelbrace, triangular type jack, hubcap remover, small tyre lever, tommy bar, plug spanner, screwdriver, tyre valve spanner, tappet feeler gauge, distributor screwdriver and gauge, feeler gauge set, axle drain plug key, grease gun and tyre pump.

From car number 848241, the following items provided a much-reduced tool kit in a black plastic tool bag with matching ties: starting handle/wheel brace, triangular type jack, hubcap remover, tommy bar, small tyre lever and a plug spanner. A supplementary tool kit, available from main dealers, contained the following items: four double-ended spanners: (⅝in × ⅜in AF, ⁷⁄₁₆in × ½in AF, ⅝in × ⅜in AF, ¹¹⁄₁₆in × ¾in AF), an adjustable 7in spanner, a tubular spanner (½in × ⁹⁄₁₆in AF), a tommy bar (⅜in diameter), 6in pliers and a cross-headed screwdriver.

EXPORT VARIATIONS

On 948cc Minor 1000 models, the established pattern of export variations continued, with flashing indicators, already an option for some export models, becoming standard specification for all export models in 1958. Cover panels were fitted to conceal redundant trafficator apertures.

The late 1950s were boom years for sales in North America. Whitewall tyres became an optional extra for export models, while other dealer-added extras available in the USA included 'Yankee' brand mirrors and Amco overrider bars. The Lucas mirrors available as an accessory for home market models did not have type approval in the USA, while Amco bars, fitted to the front and rear of saloon models, provided added protection to the grille and 'trunk' panel in the event of a light impact.

Prior to the fitting of sealed beam headlamp units for export models, the following differences applied in the bulbs fitted to the 7in headlamp units:

Type	Watts	BMC no.
RHD (except Sweden), dip left	50/40	BFS 414
LHD (except Europe), dip right	50/40	BFS 415
Europe (except France), dip vertical	45/50	BFS 410
France, dip vertical	45/40	BFS 411

For cars exported to Europe (except Sweden) from car numbers 705700 (saloons) and 696910 (Traveller), new style European headlamps were fitted. These lamps had special bulbs and front lenses which provided an asymmetrical beam to the right or left, according to regulations in the country concerned. For Sweden the change occurred for all vehicles from car number 733180. To comply with Swiss lighting arrangements, a revised number plate illumination lamp fitted with two bulbs was introduced on two-door models from car number 798693 and four-door models from car number 799519. In addition, sidelamps with white flashers were introduced for export to Switzerland at car number 796860. Sealed beam units were fitted at the works for models destined for the USA well in advance of sealed beam lamps being fitted on home market models. Improved sealed beam units were supplied on later cars for the USA; these can be identified by the figure '2' moulded into the lens at the 12 o'clock position.

Not all Morris Minors left the factory as complete vehicles. A highly profitable segment of production related to Completely Knocked Down (CKD) vehicles, supplied as parts for reassembly elsewhere. Such was the popularity of the Morris Minor that assembly plants were established all over the world. The most significant countries in terms of sustained production were the Republic of Ireland, Holland, India, South Africa, Australia and New Zealand.

The overseas producers could use local components to supplement the main body and mechanical parts. In Holland, for instance, the Molenaar Company, already established as producers of MGs, had their own suppliers for glass, tyres, paint and lighting.

A consequence of the freedom given to these subsidiary manufacturers is the variations in trim and paint specifications. This is quite clearly demonstrated on the cars assembled in New South Wales, Australia, where local paint colours were adopted and different chassis plates utilised. In Ireland, where CKD production was sustained from 1948 until the late 1960s, Brittains of Dublin supplied their completed cars with black wing piping on all models, plain trim panels on 1098cc versions, and body-coloured wheels and grille.

Not all export models, therefore, necessarily conformed to the factory specifications. Fortunately, all CKD vehicles carry specific identification plates denoting where they were assembled, a useful starting point for researching further details of local custom and practice.

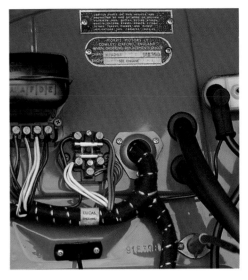

IDENTIFICATION, DATING & PRODUCTION

The arrival of the new Minor 1000, heralded as the third series of Minor, was not initially reflected in the identification code, as the original type of code continued to be used in conjunction with the Series MM and Series II style of identification plate. A minor change occurred in January 1958 when the final digit in the car number prefix indicating type of paint was discontinued.

However, by mid-1958 a new system of vehicle identification was applied on a new style of chassis plate. The new codes identified below were followed by the vehicle's chassis number, both being stamped on the plate:

MAS3 Morris A Series Engine four-door saloon, Series 3
MA2S Morris A Series Engine two-door saloon, Series 3
MAT3 Morris A Series Engine Tourer, Series 3
MAW3 Morris A Series Engine Traveller, Series 3

The above codes were followed by 'L' on cars with left-hand drive, and often by 'D' on Deluxe models.

The A-series engine fitted to the Series II had its engine number and prefix stamped on

A new style of chassis plate (above) was used from 1958, but the patent plate remained unchanged. The chassis number is also stamped into the bulkhead.

This 'anti-fumble' device (below) was offered as an accessory to overcome the problem of inadvertently operating the horn and the trafficators at the same time.

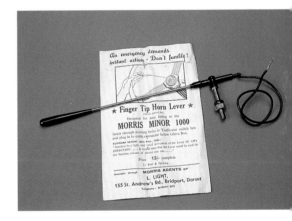

PRODUCTION FIGURES

	Two-door saloon	Four-door saloon	Convertible saloons	Traveller	Total
1956[1]	?	?	?	?	17504[2]
1957[1]	?	?	?	?	106680
1958[1]	?	?	?	?	113699
1959	54808	27411	6058	17482	105759
1960	45918	27828	4766	16804	95316
1961	28503	16038	1297	15635	61473
1962	28172	14945	898	13899	57194[3]
Total	?	?	?	?	**544048**

Notes
[1] A production breakdown of the individual body styles is not possible for these years.
[2] This was the number of 948cc models in 1956, but 52579 Morris Minors were produced altogether that year.
[3] These 1962 figures give total production for all Morris Minors in 1962, but only 43617 cars were 948cc models. A precise breakdown is not possible.

a plate fixed to the engine block, and this practice was continued on the 948cc models. For this reason, the words 'See Engine' were stamped on the new chassis plate instead of the engine number. The patents plate continued in use as before. The engine number prefix was APJM until an unspecified point in 1957, but thereafter it became 9M-U-H on high compression engines or 9M-U-L on low compression engines.

OPTIONAL EXTRAS & ACCESSORIES

There was little change to the range of optional extras available on Minor 1000 models. A radio still headed the list and a heater still had to be specified on standard models. An addition to the options was the opportunity to specify either a high or low compression engine.

For a brief period in 1959-60, a special option was offered for interior trim. Nylon cloth-covered seats were available for Deluxe versions of saloon and convertible models painted Clipper Blue, Sage Green or Smoke Grey. Blue-grey material was used on the Clipper Blue and Smoke Grey cars, while green was used on Sage Green ones. In addition to the cloth covering, grey ribbed door and seat protection strips were fitted respectively to the bottom edge of the door trim panels and on the bottom edge of the back of the front seats. An extra feature of this unique trim specification was a cloth-covered top edge for the arm rest on the rear side trim panel. It would appear that this option was not widely specified as it is rarely found on surviving cars today.

The following BMC-approved accessories were available for 948cc models in 1960 (with part number):

Boomerang wing mirror (convex), 7H9829
BMC pressurized jet fire extinguisher (5⅛in × 1⅛in), 97H752
Exterior sun visor (perspex green), 27H9678
Roof rack (rigid), 97H465
Vanity mirror, 7H9756
Windscreen washer, 17H9511
Cigarette lighter, 97H664
Fresh-air kit, incorporating heater, 8G9064
Ashtray, 17H9557
Fog lamp (SFT576), 57H5244
Long-range driving lamp (SLR576), 17H5322

Radiator blind, 27H9531
Seat covers, part numbers vary according to material
Travelling rug (all-wool tartan available for Anderson, Buchanan, Davidson of Tulloch, Dress Stewart, Macbeth, Macgregor, Macleod, Royal Stewart and Wallace), 27H9635
Supplementary tool roll, 97H524
Paint pencil (various colours)
Polished aluminium wheel discs (set of four), 97H2485
Rimbellishers
Locking petrol cap, 17H9637
Exhaust deflector, 97H600

PRODUCTION CHANGES

CHANGES BY CAR NUMBER

448801 (Oct 56)
Standard and Deluxe two- and four-door saloons, convertible and Traveller introduced, designated 'Minor 1000', 948cc engine fitted. Single-piece curved windscreen and larger rear window. Dished steering wheel. Horn and trafficator control on steering column. Glovebox lids fitted. New style rear wings on saloons and convertibles. Shorter remote control gearlever. 'Minor 1000' motif on sides of bonnet.

462458 (Dec 56)
New strengthened steering swivel pin assembly fitted.

463443 (Dec 56)
Stronger boot lid handle and lock.

487048 (saloon) (Mar 57)
485127 (Traveller)
Fuel tank enlarged from 5 to 6½ gallons.

490159 (Apr 57)
Board type headlining discontinued in Traveller.

524944 (Aug 57)
Canvas hood on convertible replaced by plastic-coated material.

549923 (intermittently) (Oct 57)
555415 (all)
Warning light with shade added to quadrant of trafficator (indicator) and horn control stalk.

552906 (Traveller) (Nov 57)
557451 (other models)
Gear lever reset and lengthened.

654750 (Sep 58)
Courtesy light switches fitted in front doors (except on convertibles).

680464 (Dec 58)
Rear spring design changed from seven ⁷⁄₃₂in leaves to five ¼in leaves, except on the Traveller.

693918 (Traveller) (Feb 59)
698137 (saloon/convertible)
Large oil-bath air cleaner replaced by early type of dry paper element cleaner.

695736 (Feb 59)
Boot stay arrangement modified on saloons and convertibles.

693589 (Traveller) (Feb 59)
695736 (saloon/convertible)
Glovebox lid fitted with liner and outer finisher.

695864 (Feb 59)
Seat covers on four-door saloon changed to broad panel style. Heater on Deluxe models fitted with Pearl Grey coloured shroud. Enlarged parcel shelf with aperture for steering column.

704254 (Traveller) (Mar 59)
705224 (four-door saloon)
705622 (two-door saloon)
Wider opening doors, self-cancelling direction indicator switch fitted to steering column (with green warning lamp on end of stalk), horn button moved to centre of steering wheel.

750470 (Aug 59)
Combined inlet and exhaust manifold. Foot space between gearbox cover and clutch pedal increased. PVC interior roof lining instead of fabric. Front passenger seat on two-door saloon and traveller modified to give better access to rear seats.

(Dec 60)
Morris Minor 1,000,000 produced as special edition of 350 cars. Features included Lilac colour, white upholstery with black piping, 'Minor 1,000,000' badging on sides of bonnet and on boot lid, special wheel rim embellishers. Car numbers of 1,000,000-1,000,349 designated out of sequence.

925448 (four-door saloon) (Aug 61)
925555 (two-door saloon)
925679 (Traveller)
926579 (convertible)
Flashing direction indicators incorporated into front and rear lamps (semaphore direction indicators discontinued). Windscreen washers fitted on Deluxe models. Seat belt anchorage points built into all models.

934673 (saloon/convertible) (Oct 61)
935632 (Traveller)
Revised seat style and new range of trim colours. Heater on Deluxe models fitted with Light Beige shroud.

939695 (Nov 61)
Glove compartment lids discontinued. Rear seat squab fastening modified on saloons and convertibles. Wiper motor and angle of wipe altered.

989679 (convertible) (Sep 62)
990283 (four-door saloon)
990288 (two-door saloon)
990289 (traveller)
Final chassis numbers for 948cc models.

CHANGES BY ENGINE NUMBER

38902 (Feb 57)
Dynamo pulley and fan belt profile changed.

283721 (Jan 59)
Solid cast rockers replaced by pressed steel rockers.

353449 (Sep 59)
SU HS carburettor introduced.

441410 (May 60)
Combined exhaust and inlet manifold (single unit).

453032 (Jun 60)
Revised timing chain cover: rubber replaces felt for oil seal.

506301 (Jan 61)
Concentric oil pump assembly replaced by Burman oil pump.

506367 (Jan 61)
Piston ring metal upgraded.

524832 (May 61)
Oil filter changed from Tecalemit to AC Purolator.

604228 (Mar 62)
Lucas distributor changed from DM2 P4 to 25D4.

618814 (Jun 62)
Water pump pulley hub modified.

BODY COLOURS: DURATION OF USE (948CC MODELS)

Colour	Introduced	Discontinued	Notes
Black	—	—	Used throughout 948cc production
Dark Green	Sep 1956 (449129)	Feb 1959 (695275)	Saloons/Convertibles/ Travellers, also on 698997 (one-off)
Clarendon Grey	—	Jan 1959 (694645)	Also on 695733 (one-off)
Birch Grey	Sep 1956 (449269)	Jan 1959 (694239)	Saloons/Convertibles/ Travellers, also on 699014 (one-off)
Sage Green	— / Feb 1959 (693808)	Mar 1959 (708537) / Mar 1959 (704301)	Saloons/Convertibles Traveller
Cream	Sep 1956 (449236)	Apr 1958 (608041)	Not used on Travellers
Turquoise	Oct 1956 (449553)	Jan 1959 (695191)	Also on 698996 (one-off) Not used on Traveller
Pale Ivory	Apr 1958 (608663)	Feb 1959 (695162)	Not used on Traveller
Frilford Grey	Jan 1959 (692882)	Jul 1960 (847831)	—
Pearl Grey	Jan 1959 (692902)	Jul 1960 (847250)	Not used on Traveller
Clipper Blue	Jan 1959 (693589) / Jan 1959 (693589)	Oct 1961 (934932) / Jul 1960 (846941)	Saloons/Convertibles Traveller
Smoke Grey	Feb 1959 (695314) / Jul 1960 (846951)	— / —	Saloons/Convertibles Traveller
Yukon Grey	Jul 1960 (847397)	Nov 1961 (939211)	—
Old English White	Jul 1960 (848109)	—	Blue trim fitted to some early cars
Porcelain Green	Jul 1960 (851256)	Oct 1961 (934714)	Not used on Traveller
Dove Grey	Oct 1961 (934892)	—	Not used on Traveller
Rose Taupe	Oct 1961 (934900)	—	—
Almond Green	Oct 1961 (935214)	—	—
Highway Yellow	Oct 1961 (936910)	Jul 1962 (979650)	Not used on Traveller
Trafalgar Blue	Aug 1962 (981731)	—	Not used on Traveller until 1098cc model

Notes
A dash indicates that colour continued on from Series II or into 1098cc period. In cases where a different starting/finishing car number or date has not been quoted for the Traveller, it may be assumed that the introduction or discontinuation of a particular colour occurred at the same time as on the saloon and convertible models.

COLOUR SCHEMES (948cc MODELS)

1956 – Feb 1959

Paint	Trim Options	Hood Options	Carpets	Headlining	Grille	Coachline	Wheels
Black★	Red★ Green★ Grey	Maroon Grey Grey	Maroon Beagle Green Black	Light Grey Light Grey Light Grey	Grey Grey Grey	Red Red Red	Birch Grey Birch Grey Birch Grey
Clarendon Grey★	Red★ Grey	Maroon Grey	Maroon Black	Light Grey Light Grey	Clarendon Grey Clarendon Grey	Red Red	Clarendon Grey Clarendon Grey
Birch Grey★	Red★ Grey	Maroon Grey	Maroon Black	Light Grey Light Grey	Birch Grey Birch Grey	Red Red	Birch Grey Birch Grey
Sage Green	Grey Green	Grey Grey	Beagle Green Beagle Green	Light Grey Light Grey	Sage Green Sage Green	Birch Grey Birch Grey	Sage Green Sage Green
Turquoise	Grey	Grey	Black	Light Grey	Turquoise	Birch Grey	Birch Grey
Cream	Red	Maroon	Maroon	Light Grey	Cream	Red	Cream
Dark Green★	Grey★	Grey	Black	Light Grey	Dark Green	Birch Grey	Birch Grey
Pale Ivory	Red	Maroon	Maroon	Light Grey	Pale Ivory	Red	Pale Ivory

Feb 1959 – Jul 1960

Paint	Trim Options	Hood Options	Carpets	Headlining	Grille	Coachline	Wheels
Frilford Grey★	Red	Maroon	Red	Pearl Grey	Pearl Grey	Red	Pearl Grey
Pearl Grey	Red	Maroon	Red	Pearl Grey	Pearl Grey	Red	Pearl Grey
Clipper Blue★	Blue-Grey	Pearl Grey	Blue	Pearl Grey	Pearl Grey	Pearl Grey	Pearl Grey
Smoke Grey	Blue-Grey	Pearl Grey	Blue	Pearl Grey	Pearl Grey	Blue	Pearl Grey
Black★	Red	Pearl Grey	Red	Pearl Grey	Pearl Grey	Red	Pearl Grey
Sage Green★	Green	Pearl Grey	Beagle Green	Pearl Grey	Pearl Grey	Pearl Grey	Pearl Grey

Jul 1960 – Oct 1961

Paint	Trim Options	Hood Options	Carpets	Headlining	Grille	Coachline	Wheels
Black★	Red	Maroon	Red	Pearl Grey	Old English White	Red	Old English White
Yukon Grey★	Red	Maroon	Red	Pearl Grey	Old English White	Red	Old English White
Smoke Grey★	Blue-Grey	Pearl Grey	Blue	Pearl Grey	Old English White	Blue	Old English White
Clipper Blue	Blue-Grey	Pearl Grey	Blue	Pearl Grey	Old English White	Old English White	Old English White
Porcelain Green	Oxford Beige	Pearl Grey	Fir Green	Pearl Grey	Old English White	Leaf Green	Old English White
Old English White★	Red	Maroon	Red	Pearl Grey	Old English White	Red	Old English White

Oct 1961 – Oct 1962

Paint	Trim Options	Hood Options	Carpets	Headlining	Grille	Coachline	Wheels
Black★	Tartan Red	Pearl Grey	Tartan Red	Light Beige	Old English White	Red	Old English White
Dove Grey	Tartan Red	Pearl Grey	Tartan Red	Light Beige	Old English White	Red	Old English White
Smoke Grey★	Blue-Grey	Pearl Grey	Blue	Light Beige	Old English White	Blue	Old English White
Almond Green★	Porcelain Green	Pearl Grey	Almond Green	Light Beige	Old English White	Porcelain Green	Old English White
Old English White★[1]	Tartan Red	Pearl Grey	Tartan Red	Light Beige	Old English White	Red	Old English White
Rose Taupe★	Tartan Red Tartan Red	Pearl Grey Maroon	Tartan Red Tartan Red	Light Beige Light Beige	Old English White Old English White	Red Red	Old English White Old English White
Highway Yellow	Blue-Grey	Pearl Grey	Blue	Light Beige	Old English White	Blue	Old English White
Trafalgar Blue	Blue-Grey	Pearl Grey	Blue	Light Beige	Old English White	Pearl Grey	Old English White

Notes

★Available as a colour and trim choice for Travellers. Models from October 1961 were fitted with duo-tone upholstery in Deluxe specification: Silver Beige panels contrasted with Tartan Red, Porcelain Green and Blue Grey. Standard specification Traveller models were fitted with black moulded rubber mats: the listing for carpets for these models is for Deluxe models.

[1]Some early Old English White cars had Blue-Grey trim.

SPECIAL OPTION VEHICLES

A number of special option Morris Minors were supplied on a contract basis to local authorities, the Ministry of Supply and other government agencies. Broadly speaking these fell into three main categories of military vehicles, police cars and disabled persons' cars.

DISABLED PERSONS' CARS

Disabled persons' cars first became available during Minor 1000 production. While you would expect these cars to have been fitted with the standard 948cc engine, the decision was taken to use the earlier 803cc overhead valve engine and Series II transmission. Consequently, the early type of disabled persons' vehicle is something of a hybrid.

Externally, these cars can be distinguished by Morris Minor badges fitted to either side of the bonnet and by the earlier Series MM and Series II boot badge complete with reflector. Internally, the differences were confined to the carpet, which of necessity had to be similar to the Series II style to take account of the early type of gearbox cover, and to the seats, which were specially adapted and mounted on sliding runners to allow for easier access and adjustment.

Later Minor 1000 disabled persons' vehicles were of more conventional specification in that they were fitted with the same 1098cc engine and other mechanical parts as standard vehicles. Differences were confined mainly to the interior, with plain door and side trims, fully adjustable front seats mounted on sliding runners, and provision for a fire extinguisher to be fitted. Special options included front seats which swivelled outwards through 90°, wider opening doors hinged specially so that they fit flush against the front wing, and fully reclining front seats. Disabled vehicles were always standard two-door saloons and all additional fittings – including hand controls – were ex-factory options.

POLICE CARS

Two-door saloons were supplied to the police as Panda cars in the final years of 1098cc production. For most cars, the livery was a two-tone combination of Police white (doors and roof forward of the B posts) and Bermuda Blue. The seat upholstery, door trim, side panels and carpets were usually black, but some cars featured red trim.

A distinctive feature of Panda cars is a special zipped headlining. This was ostensibly to allow access to the police sign fitted on the roof, but enterprising constables used it as an extra storage place for their sandwiches!

Not all cars supplied to the police were in this livery. Some were plain white with black

Police Panda cars were supplied to special order. Painted in Bermuda Blue and Police White, they had unusual trim combinations. Red or black were the most common colours for seats and trim.

A zipped headlining was a unique feature on police vehicles.

upholstery and carpets. Other models, including vans, Travellers and four-door saloons, were supplied in Trafalgar Blue. Additional special options included the use of an 11AC alternator and specially calibrated accurate speedometers. Police cars were typically supplied complete with two wing-mounted exterior mirrors of the sprung 'swing-back' type and inertia reel front seat belts, and were often fitted with diaphragm-type front seats, the better to support constabulary weight!

ARMED SERVICES VEHICLES

Identification plates on military vehicles differed significantly from standard. The plate (below right), normally fixed to the bulkhead, was fitted to a Traveller supplied to the army, while a further identification plate (below left) was attached to the passenger side glovebox lid on later models.

The armed services used a number of Morris Minor models as part of their fleet of utility vehicles. The most popular model was the Traveller, which was supplied in batches to special contracts for the Army, Navy and RAF. Special features of these versatile vehicles were the plain door trims and side panels, the absence of floor and side coverings in the rear loading compartment, and the use of a one-piece rubber mat for the cabin floor.

Most Army vehicles were painted in Army Bronze Green and had a complementary Porcelain Green interior, but later versions had Autumn Leaf or black interiors. Unlike standard production models, wheels and grilles were painted body colour. Some Army Travellers were left-hand drive vehicles fitted with steering locks, for use by the British Army in Germany. RAF vehicles were RAF Blue Grey and Navy vehicles were Dark Blue, both having light blue, red or, later on, black interiors. As with disabled persons' vehicles, provision was made for fitting a fire extinguisher to the nearside scuttle.

Exceptions to the standard services trim specification applied to 'special duties' vehicles. Bomb disposal vehicles were characterised by their red wings and vehicles operating on airfields were distinguished by a yellow band painted around the middle.

Additional distinguishing features of these vehicles are the special identification plates fitted to the bulkhead and in some cases to the interior. These provide specific information relating to the service they were supplied for and include details of the type of vehicle.

Features peculiar to the disabled persons' version include plain door trims, a fire extinguisher and front seats mounted on special runners to allow for easy adjustment.

CAR UTILITY – 4×2 – MORRIS 1000
CONTRACT Nº WV9530/BL(A-M)129
CODE Nº   1140–0659
NATO CODE 2310–99–807–0441
CHASSIS Nº 1286868

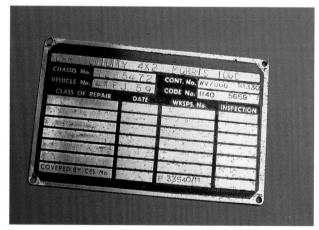

MINOR MILLION

This limited edition Minor Million is one of 350 produced. Although they were all finished in this delicate shade of lilac, initial thoughts were that they should be painted silver.

Although it differs in detail and colour, the special interior of the Minor Million followed the same basic pattern of the normal production models in December 1960.

The new Minor 1000 was a resounding success. Sales in the first full year topped 100,000 and this was matched in succeeding years up to 1960. This was boom time for the 'World's Supreme Small Car' and history was in the making. An early prediction by the management at Morris Motors Ltd that the new post-war Morris might be good for 250,000 units was looking decidedly off

beam. Towards the end of 1960, the statisticians estimated that the figure of one million Morris Minors would soon be surpassed. This really would be a motoring milestone, as a million units of a particular model had never before been built in Britain.

A limited edition Morris Minor, the Minor Million, was produced to mark the event. In keeping with the swinging sixties,

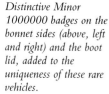

Distinctive Minor 1000000 badges on the bonnet sides (above, left and right) and the boot lid, added to the uniqueness of these rare vehicles.

it was finished in a delicate shade of lilac and special features included a unique interior with leather seats finished in off-white with black piping, black carpets, black door sealing rubbers and a light grey headlining. Special commemorative Minor 1,000,000 badges were fitted to the boot lid and bonnet sides where ordinarily Minor 1000 badges would have been placed. Further distinctive features included cream-coloured (or possibly Old English White, according to one school of thought) wheels, matching grille bars and special chrome wheel rim embellishers.

A total of 349 replicas of the Minor Million were produced. The chassis numbers were allocated out of sequence and the millionth Minor with chassis number 1,000,000 was assembled on 22 December 1960. This car was used extensively for publicity during the first six months of 1961 and was registered with the number 1 MHU. The other 349 cars were distributed to main dealers throughout the UK, the Channel Islands, Europe and North America, 30 of the batch being left-hand drive.

An added bonus to all the publicity which justifiably surrounded this landmark was a successful outcome to a competition to find the oldest surviving Morris Minor. The lucky owner – provided he or she liked lilac – would be given a Minor Million as long as his or her car had completed 100,000 miles. It was in this way that the first Morris Minor, with chassis number SMM 501 and registered NWL 576, was rediscovered in Sheffield, returned to the BMC workshops and restored to its former glory. It still survives and is now on display at the Heritage Motor Centre at Gaydon in Warwickshire.

Wheel rim embellishers were an additional feature on the Minor Million.

MORRIS MINOR 1000 (1962-71)

The final major update to the Morris Minor was a progressive affair. The first stage, undertaken in September 1962, concentrated on further updating of the mechanical side and resulted from rationalisation within BMC in the use of the 1098cc A-series engine, which also powered the Austin A40 and Austin Healey Sprite. The Minor 1000, as it was still known, was otherwise unaltered, the outer bodyshell, body panels, exterior trim and interior specifications remaining as they had been for the 948cc models.

Further advances introduced in October 1963 for the 1964 model year included the provision of effective combined indicator and brake lamps at the rear, combined side/indicator lamps at the front, improvements to the windscreen washers and wipers, and the addition of a nearside exterior door lock. This last feature, incidentally, gave left-hand drive owners an externally lockable driver's door for the first time, after the 15-year aberration of having an exterior lock only on the passenger door.

The last of the big changes came in October 1964. A revised interior and modified fascia combined to add the final distinctive characteristics to these 1098cc models and end what can only be described as a lengthy gestation period. However well-intentioned and necessary the improvements were, the fact that the Minor had been around for quite a while was beginning to be reflected in the sales figures, competition from up and coming cars in the same stable taking its toll. Sales of the Mini and the Austin/Morris 1100 were on the up, while those of the Minor were struggling to reach even a third of their 100,000 a year level in the heady days.

The Minor's new lease of life was short-lived, and when BMC gave way to British Leyland in 1968 the writing was on the wall. Amazingly, the Morris Minor survived for a while despite the fact that profit margins were tiny. The popular convertible was the first to go in 1969, followed by the saloons in 1970. The versatile Traveller struggled on

Mike Taylor's 1966 four-door saloon in Smoke Grey highlights some distinctive features, such as windscreen wipers working in tandem, combined sidelight/indicator lamp units at the front, and a revised B-post pressing at the point where trafficators would have been fitted on earlier models.

Harry Cook has owned this Almond Green Traveller from new. Meticulous care and attention to detail have ensured that the original ash has been preserved and the rest of the car remains in showroom condition.

This angle of Keith Fletcher's 1966 Almond Green convertible shows how the enlarged rear window on all Minor 1000 hoods allowed much better rearward visibility with the hood up. The hood design is authentic but the colour is non-standard.

This early 1098cc Minor 1000 is one of the 'transition' vehicles. These rear lights were carried on from 948cc models until October 1963.

until 1971 with production taking place at Adderley Park, Birmingham from July 1969.

In all, 1,619,958 Morris Minors were built over 22 years. The model's demise marked the end of an era in British motoring.

BODY & CHASSIS

The main bodyshell remained largely unchanged for all models in the final years of production. A detail addition to the main bodyshell was the provision of seat belt mounting points, which were first fitted in 1961 to the last of the 948cc models and were subsequently amended on 1098cc models. Initially the seat belts themselves were an optional extra, but legislation in June 1964 led to static belts being fitted by dealers as a matter of course, and inertia reel belts being offered as an approved accessory. When seat belts became mandatory on 1 January 1971, static belts were fitted as standard at the factory.

The boot lid was slightly altered in order to improve the arrangement for the boot support mechanism. From 1964, a new telescopic self-locking support meant that the boot could be opened and locked in position in a single action. This was a big improvement on the earlier method (part of the original design), which entailed placing the support prop in position on opening and

Conventional windscreen wipers which work in tandem were a welcome innovation on 1098cc models and provide an increased area of wipe.

then repositioning it in the secured position prior to closing. Though simple and reasonably effective, the old design meant that the boot lid could be forced back over the roof panel in windy weather!

A small amendment occurred on the left-hand outer door skin pressing, which was altered to accommodate the new locking arrangement with an external key-operated lock.

BODY TRIM

So far as items of exterior trim were concerned, it was very much a matter of 'as you were' when the 1098cc models were intro-

The front of the 1098cc models remained unchanged except for new combined indicator and sidelight units. On late American export models the whole of the lens cover is frosted; because these items are now in short supply, the contrasting European alternatives are pressed into service on an increasing number of surviving American cars.

This narrow pinstripe coachline (below) is original and correct for this Smoke Grey car. The MINOR 1000 badge on each side of the bonnet was introduced at the start of 948cc production, replacing the earlier MORRIS MINOR wording.

The discontinuation of trafficators, which had occurred on the home market models late in 948cc production, meant that the B post was modified on four-door saloons. This integral pressing (right) was a neater solution than the blanking plates added to 948cc export models fitted with indicators prior to the disappearance of trafficators for the home market.

duced. During the course of production, however, small changes to the bonnet flash and the windscreen surround did occur. Having been a composite item, the bonnet flash became a single chromed Mazak casting, with the 'M' motif highlighted on a painted red background. The windscreen surround was altered from a two-piece alloy fitting to a single plastic-covered, chrome-effect extrusion which fitted into the windscreen rubber. The use of outer finishers was dispensed with when this change was introduced, later in production in 1966.

LIGHTING

The major change to the Minor's exterior, and the one which most readily distinguishes the majority of 1098cc models from all others, was the introduction in October 1963 of large combined indicator/stop/tail light units at the rear and combined indicator/side light units at the front. Long overdue, these rear lights replaced the 'stop gap' relay system for 948cc cars described in the previous chapter; this earlier system carried forward to early 1098cc 'transition' vehicles and remained in use until October 1963.

The Autocar caught the mood when it described the new lights as 'businesslike' and observed that they 'were meant to be seen'. This latter observation could not have been made with conviction for previous lighting arrangements, particularly at the rear. The jury was still out on the Traveller – which for obvious reasons could not aspire to such a tidy arrangement and had to make do with

This rear view of the Traveller shows the easy access to the rear loading area. The rear doors are held open by a special self-locking mechanism. The spare wheel compartment is concealed by an easily removable black wooden board held in position by two wooden fillets.

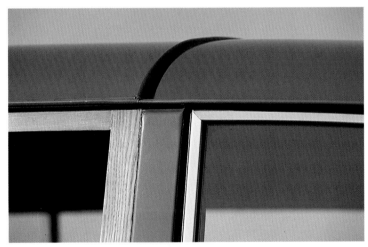

All Traveller body panels are steel forward of the roof sealing rubber (above). Rearwards of it, all panels are aluminium with the exception of the rear wings. Stainless steel door window surrounds are used on Travellers.

The side windows on 1098cc Travellers have a revised type of catch which operates in the vertical position (above). The two side panels below the waist rail are aluminium. Matching body colour wing piping is placed between the three-sectioned wooden wheelarch panel and the steel rear wing.

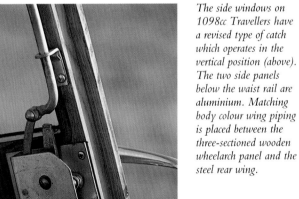

Rear bumpers on the Traveller are unique to that model and secured by black-painted bumper brackets.

The internal locking mechanism for the Traveller's rear doors. The exterior handle points downwards when the doors are closed. The interior panel on each rear door is aluminium.

Door hinges painted in body colour are a feature of all Traveller models. This is the late style of rear light treatment, with two apertures in the rear pillars. Separate stop/tail, indicator and reflector fittings were standard on all Travellers following the introduction of integral indicator/sidelight units at the front.

This is the familiar combined indicator/ sidelight unit (right) introduced for 1098cc Minors, together with a sealed beam headlamp as fitted from 1966. This car is reputed to be the very first home market model fitted with sealed beam headlamps.

The front posts of the Traveller's ash frame are located by cross-headed bolts which fasten on to caged nuts on the B post. Door handles on Traveller models are the same as those used on two-door saloons.

separate indicator lamps which matched the style of the existing stop/tail lamps.

A further lighting update occurred in 1966 when sealed beam headlamp units were fitted as standard. This long-overdue improvement brought to an end the long-standing use of 7in pre-focus units on home market models. A final detail change saw the introduction of a fuse for the sidelight circuit.

WEATHER EQUIPMENT

There were no significant changes to the design of the weather equipment fitted to the 1098cc convertibles during the period

This businesslike style of rear lamps arrived for 1098cc models in October 1963. Also shown here is the authentic fuel filler cap arrangement with a securing chain.

When securing the hood in the raised position, care has to be taken to ensure that the overlap at the edge of the hood embraces the window frame, particularly at the curve of the rear side windows.

This interior view (below) of the hood in the raised position shows the obtrusive appearance of the hood sticks. All 948cc and 1098cc Minor 1000 models have a larger rear window than on previous hoods.

Once released, by unscrewing the two wing bolts on the header rail, the hood should be raised upwards and backwards as illustrated here. It is not, as some suggest, an easy one-person operation.

When the hood sticks sit in the folded position, care needs to be taken to ensure that the hood, including the rear window, is not trapped.

Instructions in the driver's handbook recommend drawing the hood materials clear of the hood sticks prior to folding in the corners and rolling it back over the sticks. Having done this the loose-fitting hood cover can be secured by the press stud fastenings.

The final style of interior fitted to the Minor 1000 from October 1964 is shown to good effect in this 1966 convertible. Heat-formed fluted panels on seats, door trims and rear side trim panels were common to both Standard and Deluxe models. Note the position of the seat belt mounting bracket on most two-door saloons and convertibles; later versions had a welded mounting forward of this position.

1962-69, but the colour was now Pearl Grey only (except for a few later models, as indicated in the 'Colour Schemes' table later in this chapter).

INTERIOR TRIM

At the outset, the absence of any change to the interior trim was understandable, given the frequency with which new styles had been introduced on the 948cc Minor 1000. The plain single colour upholstery for Standard models and contrasting two-tone for Deluxe models continued in use up to October 1964. Headlinings and sunvisors were light beige, while carpets were unchanged in style, cut and fitting, with green, red and blue colours dominating.

October 1964 brought the Minor's last major interior trim update. Retaining fluted panels was an element of continuity, but a new appearance was created by a different process and different materials. Heat-formed vinyl panels were used on door trims and on the seat cushions and backrests. Eight fluted panels were incorporated into the base and backrest of the front seats, this pattern extending to ten fluted panels for each half of the rear seat base and backrest. The various door trim panels used on saloons, convertibles and Travellers had continuous fluted panels on the bottom half, this treatment

Door window frames and opening quarterlight frames were painted on two-door saloon and convertible models. Adjustment for the opening quarterlight is by a chrome-plated screw. In style and operation the door handles remain as they were at the very start of Morris Minor production, while the vinyl-covered door pull dates back to the late Series MM period.

continuing to the rear side panel on two-door saloons and convertibles. However, the Traveller's rear side panels, with integral arm rest, remained plain, as did the side panels fitted in the rear compartment of Deluxe model Travellers. Up to car number 935633, rear side panels had not been fitted to the Traveller, leaving the wheelarch exposed. From this car number, late 948cc Deluxe

A fixed-back passenger seat (below) replaced the previous 'tilt-and-fold' design on saloon, convertible and Traveller models from October 1964. The chrome-plated door striker plate and alloy 'easy action' internal door lock mechanism are visible on the edge of the door.

The hinged rear seat base on this Traveller (above) has been folded forward to reveal the locating plate for the seat back and the original sound deadening underfelt beneath the seat base.

Using the seat belts in Traveller models was made more convenient by the positioning of the upper mounting high on the B post.

The material used in the covered loading area on the Minor 1000 Traveller proved to be very durable and hard-wearing. This is the beautifully preserved original material supplied with this Traveller, but replacement materials are available.

The tunnel-mounted ashtray on Minor 1000s is housed within an outer casing secured by four self-tapping screws (above left). The change to a black crash pad on the parcel shelf in October 1964 was accompanied by the use of black swivel ashtrays (above right) which included a metal heat shield as part of the design.

The interior light in Traveller models is positioned to the rear of the cabin, but on saloons it is sited just in front of the interior mirror. Door-operated courtesy lights activated by contact switches positioned in the A posts are a feature of all post-1958 Minors except for the convertibles, which had no interior light and used a rubber blanking grommet to cover the switch aperture on each A post.

The final layout of the dashboard for 1098cc models saw the reappearance in October 1964 of a glovebox lid on the passenger side. The black heater cover panel, parcel shelf, steering wheel, steering column and speedometer face — all new features introduced at the same time — toned in well with all the body colours and provided a welcome contrast.

models and all 1098cc Deluxe models acquired a matching plain side panel and the wheelarch was covered with a durable, felt-backed, PVC-covered, specially-shaped grey matting.

The basic construction of the seat frames remained the same, as did the practice of using rubberised seat webbing fixed to the frame by wire clips. However, fixed-back front seats were introduced in October 1964 and remained for the rest of production. Other amendments at the same time included the use of a black crash pad on the front edge of the parcel shelf, a change in the design of the door pull escutcheon, and revised sun visors and sun visor mountings. Instead of being fixed, the new 'crushable' sun visors each had a swivel mounting which allowed them to be used over the side windows; two white plastic locating hooks retained the visors in the normal position. A passenger side sun visor was still a Deluxe specification at this time.

During the rest of production, the range of interior trim colours expanded: the various combinations are detailed in the 'Colour Schemes' section later in this chapter.

For a short time towards the end of production, fully reclining seats became an optional extra. These are very rare indeed and few are ever seen!

DASHBOARD & INSTRUMENTS

Continuity was maintained on early 1098cc models by the use of a central bronze-faced

speedometer flanked by two open glove-boxes, and by the extended use of push/pull control switches. *The Autocar* recorded that the Minor was one of the last cars to use a separate starter and ignition system, but some solace was offered in the concession that more illustrious marques such as Jaguar and Rolls-Royce employed a similar system.

Amendments to the control switches included the addition of a new under-fascia switch for the standard Wingard windscreen washers. The system was subsequently updated when the early washer bottle mounting bracket with two wire securing clips was replaced by a revised bracket with two sprung metal retaining clips.

A significant change to the fascia occurred as part of the general interior update in October 1964, when a final flirtation with the idea of glovebox lids led to a 'half and half' arrangement. The driver's side compartment remained open but the one on the

An anodised backing panel and chrome finishers complemented the new style of speedometer on all but the earliest 1098cc models. On a late vehicle fitted with a steering column lock, a chrome blanking plate would cover the space occupied by the ignition key.

SPEEDOMETER IDENTIFICATION (1098cc MODELS)

Identification code	Colour	Mph/kph	Model	Chassis numbers
SN4477/80	Bronze	Mph	Two-door Four-door Convertible Traveller	990290-1082279 990290-1082283 990290-1082716 990290-1082536
SN4477/31	Bronze	Kph	Two-door Four-door Convertible Traveller	990289-1082279 990289-1082283 990289-1082716 990289-1082536
SN4419/04	Black	Mph	Two-door Four-door Convertible Traveller	1082280-1203563 1082284-1203563 1082717-1203563 1082537-1203563
SN4423/06	Black	Mph	All models	1203563 onwards
SN4419/12	Black	Mph	All models	Available throughout with special option Dunlop SP 145-14N tyres
SN4419/05	Black	Kph	Two-door Four-door Convertible Traveller	1082280-1206703 1082284-1206703 1082717-1206703 1082537-1206703
SN4423/07	Black	Kph	All models	1206703 onwards

passenger side gained a metal lid painted body colour. Central to the fascia changes – quite literally – was the speedometer. It now sported a black circular dial with white numerals, and incorporated an odometer, fuel gauge and warning lights for headlamp main beam, oil and ignition. It was tastefully set against a contrasting anodised aluminium panel and flanked by two upright chrome finishers. During the remainder of production, the speedometer was twice updated, first when kph calibration was included on the dial's inner ring for home market models, and later when an oil filter warning light was included. A detailed reference list of the speedometers fitted during production appears in the accompanying table.

This October 1964 update also included improvements to the central switches. At last a proper key-operated starting system appeared, and the long-standing pull/push switches were replaced by much simpler toggle switches for lights and wipers. The extra space created by the new ignition system allowed the windscreen washer control to move to the main console. The position, identification and operation of the choke control remained unchanged. The

use of black switches improved the general appearance of the fascia and provided consistency, for the speedometer, steering wheel, steering column, parcel shelf, crash pad, heater cover and ashtrays were all black. Controls which remained in the same position included the fascia illumination switch (as inconspicuous as ever), the floor-mounted dipswitch and the column-mounted indicator switch with its integral green light.

A detailed description of the heating system appears later in the 'Cooling System' section. A transitional period in 1963-64 allowed a choice of two types of heater, so early 1098cc cars can be fitted with either the Smiths recirculatory heater (with a variable rheostat) or the later 2.8kw heater (with a three-position lever vent control and a simple on/off fan switch). Eventually in October 1964, as part of the general interior update, this later heater was fitted as standard.

From January 1971, steering column locks were used on some Travellers. On these models a chrome blanking disc was fitted to the control panel over the space for the conventional key-operated ignition. Steering column locks were found earlier on certain export models.

ENGINE

The choice of the 1098cc engine resulted mainly from a decision to maximise the use of this version of the A-series family throughout the BMC range, rather than any specific requirement to update the Morris Minor. Even if it was not a particularly inspired choice, it did provide a welcome increase in power output and gave improved performance. The essential features of the previous 948cc A-series engine were retained, albeit in a new cast-iron block. The bore and stroke were increased to 64.6mm and 83.7mm respectively, and the compression ratio was increased slightly to 8.5:1.

Taken with changes in the gearbox and rear axle ratios, the result was an increase of 30 per cent in maximum power and a reduction of almost 6sec in the 0-60mph time. This fact was significant because it put the Minor on a competitive footing with more modern rivals, as *The Autocar* pointed out when it compared the Minor with two stablemates (Austin A40 MkII and Morris 1100) and two rivals (Vauxhall Viva and Ford Anglia Super). A maximum speed of over 80mph was possible with a following wind, although the road test recorded 77mph. The

This is the 1098cc A-series engine. Features to note include the 'elephant's trunk' fresh air ducting used with the improved 2.8kw heater, the range of advice and caution labels fitted, and the last in a long line of air cleaner assemblies in the form of a Cooper paper element type.

positive advantage was that the larger engine allowed such speeds to be maintained with less effort and in a manner which allowed the engine to sound less busy.

Modifications to the internal components of the 1098cc engine included a strengthened crankshaft and the use of solid-skirt pistons with plain internally-chamfered and chrome-plated top compression rings, and taper-faced second and third rings. There was also an option of a low compression (7.5:1) version.

Consistency was maintained for the remainder of production with the use of green paint for the engine block, sump cover and rocker cover. Whereas earlier models had the distinctive black-on-silver Morris identity label and Weslake engine patent plate riveted to the cover, these were glued on 1098cc engines.

COOLING SYSTEM

The principal features of the cooling system remained unchanged throughout production, and at first all the components were identical to the 948cc models. The same Smiths recirculatory heater continued to be fitted (but still only as an option on Standard cars) and had a fresh air facility included.

From April 1963, however, significant changes to the radiator cowling and

bulkhead allowed a new type of heater to be fitted as an optional kit, but it later became standard. Consequently, from car number 1039564 the radiator cowling and bulkhead assembly each had an aperture to enable fresh air ducting to be installed. Cars not fitted with a heater had a metal blanking disc secured on the inside of the bulkhead by four self-tapping screws.

When fitted, the components of the new heater assembly, particularly the black fresh air ducting, dominated the engine bay. Other associated plumbing was routed differently, following a line on the engine's spark plug side. A welcome development was the ability to operate the water valve mounted on top of the engine block from inside the car by means of a push/pull control located beneath the fascia. Previously it had been necessary to adjust this valve *in situ* by turning a tap in the engine bay in order to regulate the supply of hot water to the heater.

FUEL SYSTEM

With the exception of yet another new style of air cleaner assembly, the fuel system remained as before. The SU HS2 carburettor continued to be used in conjunction with the SU fuel pump type L, and the tank capacity remained at 6½ gallons.

A new design feature linked to the Cooper

A Lucas 11 AC alternator was fitted to some special option vehicles (such as police cars) and some late Traveller models. The engine identification code 10V denotes whether this was part of the original specification.

paper element air cleaner aided the operation of the carburettor in winter. The facility to change the position of the air intake meant that it could be positioned adjacent to the exhaust manifold, so that warmed air would prevent carburettor icing. Owners were advised on the procedure in the driver's handbook and encouraged to change the position for summer and winter motoring.

It almost goes without saying that the air cleaner assembly was painted black, but it did carry a distinctive brand name label to identify it as having a Cooper element.

EXHAUST SYSTEM

The entire exhaust system remained unchanged, even down to the distinctive resonance encountered on overrun – still a certain way to recognise the presence of a Minor today!

ELECTRICS

Although the 12-volt positive earth electrical system continued in use on the 1098cc Minors, significant changes to some of the components occurred during production. At the outset the factory-supplied battery was the same BT7A (rated at 43Ah) used on the 948cc models, but by 1964 this had changed to a D9 battery. Towards the end of production in 1970, an addendum to the driver's handbook listed

no fewer than three basic types – D9 or DZ9, A9 or AZ9 and A7 or AZ7 – as being available. Batteries designated with a Z were dry-charged for export models.

On D9/DZ9 batteries, access to the cells for routine maintenance was by a removable plastic 'manifold' imprinted with the Lucas brand name. On A9/AZ9 'Pacemaker' batteries, the manifold/vent cover was not detachable, but a hinged arrangement allowed the vent cover to be first lifted vertically and then tilted to one side to allow access to a specially-designed trough. After topping up, the replacement of the vent cover automatically distributed the correct amount of water to each cell. An additional feature of this type of battery was its translucent casing. Whereas the D9/DZ9 and A9/AZ9 batteries were rated at 40Ah, the A7/AZ7 was only 30Ah.

Two types of starter motor were used on 1098cc models, the long-standing Lucas M35G type being replaced on later models by the updated M35J. Apart from the brush cover band fitted to the M35G, the units are externally similar, but differ internally in two main respects. The M35G has a peripheral contact commutator on which the bushes bear from the side, while the M35J has a face commutator where the bushes bear on the end plate. A further difference related to the earthing arrangement. On the M35J the field windings are earthed to the starter yoke, while the brush box end assembly and the commutator end plate bushes are fully insulated. This contrasts with the earlier type where the field windings are insulated from the yoke and the end plate bushes are earthed directly to the end plate.

Other amendments to the components included the introduction of Lucar snap connectors in place of screw ones on the voltage regulator and fuses, the phasing out of the nickel-plated relay unit, and a switch in position for the flasher unit from the inner flitch panel to the bulkhead.

The dynamo was updated to the C40:1 type. Late in production a conventional Lucas 11 AC alternator with a separate control box was used on those models fitted with an engine designated 10V-190-E-H, particularly Police and Army vehicles.

Existing components which continued in use were the SU type L fuel pump, the LA12 coil, the 25D4 distributor and Champion N5 14mm sparking plugs. The DR3A wiper motor also continued in use, but the clap hands action was superseded in 1963 by a more conventional parallel wipe pattern.

A new horn was also fitted to 1098cc Minors. Still of the Windtone type and located in the same position, it had a more compact design than the previous domed shape. A revised mounting bracket was fitted from car number 1039596.

TRANSMISSION

The mechanical updates on the 1098cc models included significant changes in the transmission. The extended use of the 6¼in clutch plate eventually came to an end when a larger 7¼in Borg & Beck dry-plate clutch was employed. Its use in conjunction with an improved four-speed gearbox provided better control and considerably reduced a tendency for the clutch to judder.

The 1098cc gearbox is easily distinguished from previous units by its ribbed outer casing, which provided increased strength. Internally, its operation was improved by the adoption of baulk ring synchromesh in place of the previous cone type, a move designed to combat excessive synchromesh wear. This also had the benefit of further improving the gear change itself, a fact confirmed by an enthusiastic road-tester who described its ease of operation by using the analogy 'knife through butter'.

The propshaft and universal joints remained unchanged and the use of the sliding joint in the gearbox continued. The general construction of the rear axle also remained unchanged except for the position of the oil filler. On 1098cc models this was positioned on the rearward part of the axle casing whereas on previous 948cc models it had been on the differential unit.

A revised axle ratio was standard on all models. This was increased to 4.22:1 and gave improved performance at higher speeds, but the old 4.55:1 ratio remained as an option. The overall gear ratios were as follows:

	4.22:1 axle	4.55:1 axle
First	15.28:1	16.51:1
Second	9.17:1	9.88:1
Third	5.95:1	6.42:1
Top	4.22:1	4.55:1
Reverse	19.66:1	21.22:1

SUSPENSION

The tried and tested suspension layout remained unchanged on the last series of Minors, but was criticised when the 1098cc models were first road-tested. Although state

The jacking points, plugged by rubber blanking pieces, are attached to the ends of the central crossmember.

of the art in 1948, the ride by 1964 was described as 'firm and lively' and the fact was recognised that advances in the understanding of suspension behaviour and technology had overtaken the Minor – a veiled reference no doubt to the Hydrolastic suspension employed on the Austin/Morris 1100. The finish applied to all suspension components remained unchanged.

STEERING

Like the suspension, the rack and pinion steering system remained the same as before. Change was confined to the steering wheel, which was updated in October 1964. In a concession to safety, the steering wheel was redesigned and became a two-spoke dished wheel with a centre horn push featuring the 'M' motif on a red background. The steering wheel and column were black.

BRAKES

Improvements to the braking system accompanied the increase in engine power on 1098cc models. Although efficient, the brakes on previous Minors were often regarded as adequate rather than exceptional. The introduction of larger front brake drums (increased from 7in to 8in) coupled with a reduction in the internal diameter of the rear wheel cylinders (from ⅞in to ¹³⁄₁₆in) and the master cylinder (from ⅞in to ¾in) helped to silence the critics. More important, the collective result was a substantial improvement in the overall efficiency of the brakes in terms of balance within the system, ease of operation and overall stopping power.

The handbrake continued to be painted black and operated as before, its white plastic release button being a notable characteristic.

Fortunately, few owners have suffered the fate of one unlucky contemporary road tester who found himself in the firing line when the spring-loaded release mechanism in the handbrake launched a barrage of internal components around the car!

A figure describing the internal diameter of the master cylinder is cast into the side of the unit – useful when distinguishing between early and late types at autojumbles. The respective Lockheed part numbers are 88702 for 948cc and earlier Minors, 4225-453 for 1098cc cars.

WHEELS & TYRES

The same style of 14in pressed steel disc wheels used on the 948cc Minor 1000 continued for 1098cc models. The established practice of painting the wheels Old English White continued until October 1967, after which date all vehicles left the factory with silver coloured wheels. Stainless steel and chrome-plated hub caps were available for use on all models. Doubt surrounds the precise distinction in their application to models leaving the factory, but chrome-plated hub caps are likely to have been part of the Deluxe specification. Restorers tend to favour the use of chrome-plated hub caps because of their superior finish.

Tyres changed with the introduction of the new 1098cc models: 5.20-14 Dunlop crossply tyres were now fitted as standard and towards the end of production these changed from C41 to D75. Post-1968, radial tyres were offered as an optional extra, Dunlop SP 145-14 being the usual variety. Recommended pressures for crossply tyres remained unchanged, but for radial tyres the suggested pressures were 24lb sq/in front and 26lb sq/in rear.

The standard tool kit for Minor 1000 models had a distinctive red jack and combined wheelbrace and starting handle.

It is easier to use the jack with the door open, as full rotation of the jack handle is otherwise difficult.

A starting handle — this is the last type used — remained a characteristic feature of the Morris Minor until the end of production.

TOOL KIT

The trend started with the 948cc models in supplying a reduced tool kit as standard continued. The following items were included in the black plastic tool bag with matching ties: combined wheelbrace/ starting handle, jack (triangular type), hub disc remover, 9in tommy bar and box spanner.

A supplementary tool kit, supplied in a waterproof canvas roll and available from main dealers and distributors, comprised the following items: six spanners ($\frac{3}{8}$in × $\frac{3}{8}$in AF, $\frac{7}{16}$in × $\frac{1}{2}$in AF, $\frac{1}{2}$in × $\frac{9}{16}$in AF, $\frac{9}{16}$in × $\frac{5}{8}$in AF, $\frac{11}{16}$in × $\frac{13}{16}$in AF, $\frac{3}{4}$in × $\frac{7}{8}$in AF), pair of 6in pliers, tommy bar (7in × $\frac{3}{8}$in), tubular spanner ($\frac{1}{2}$in × $\frac{9}{16}$in AF) and two screwdrivers.

EXPORT VARIATIONS

Few changes occurred on 1098cc export models, diminishing sales in the USA perhaps contributing in part to this. By 1967, in fact, emission control regulations effectively killed off sales of Morris Minors in the USA. Concessions to American regulations still applied, and upon the introduction of the larger combined rear light/brake/indicator units for all models in 1963, an all-red lens was supplied for North American saloons. Traveller models had twin red lenses fitted at the rear as standard, and all US versions had clear front sidelight lenses without the amber indicator section fitted to home market models. After the change from the 'clap hands' action of the wipers, left-hand drive wipers operated in tandem as a mirror image of the right-hand drive pattern. Laminated windscreens were fitted to all 1098cc models exported to the USA. Final modifications to late US models with 10ME engines included positive crank-case ventilation incorporating a specially

Left-hand drive models mirror all the major features of the dashboard, but metric markings mean that the black-faced speedometer of this 1098cc model reads to 140kph.

designed breather control valve.

North America excepted, exports continued to the end of production and efforts were made to comply with specific items of legislation so that sales could continue. In Holland, Belgium and France, for example, requirements relating to the braking system necessitated the fitting of a separate plastic brake fluid reservoir on the bulkhead. A steering lock was fitted for certain European markets, including Germany and Sweden.

IDENTIFICATION, DATING & PRODUCTION

Vehicle information continued to be recorded in the same way on the chassis plate on the bulkhead and on the plate attached to the engine block. The 1098cc series of vehicles were designated Series V, Series IV being omitted as this designation had been given to the Morris Mini-Minor. The use of patent plates was discontinued during 1098cc production. Later 1098cc vehicles have a letter suffix after the car number indicating assembly plant, either 'M' for Cowley or 'F' for Adderley Park in Birmingham.

For car numbers 990290 to 1248581 (with the exception of the 1,000,000 to 1,000,349 batch allocated out of sequence for the 948cc Minor Million), the engine number prefix is 10 MA-U-H (High compression) or 10 MA-U-L (Low compression). Some North

American export models with positive crankcase ventilation have prefix 10ME-U-H and are marked NA in the production records. In addition, they have much lower engine numbers than other cars built around the same time.

Car numbers from 1248582 (March 1969) to the end of production have a new engine number prefix of 10V-189-E-H (High compression) or 10V-189-E-L (Low compression) for cars fitted with dynamos. Some later vehicles supplied to the police and the armed services had an alternator fitted and are distinguished by a prefix of 10V-190-E-H (High compression) or 10V-190-E-L (Low compression).

A heater booster was fitted as standard to export models destined for colder climates, in this case Scandinavia.

A rear window heater was only available as an accessory. This Smiths version was particularly suited for use on Traveller models.

BODY COLOURS: DURATION OF USE (1098cc MODELS)

Colour	Introduced[1]	Discontinued[2]	Notes
Black	—	Nov 1970 (1287903)	Saloon
		Jul 1969 (1257121)[3]	Traveller
Smoke Grey	—	Nov 1970 (1288358)	Saloon
		Jul 1969 (1257326)[3]	Traveller
Old English White	—	Jan 1968 (1208986)	
Dove Grey	—	Jan 1968 (1208363)	Not used on Traveller
Rose Taupe	—	Dec 1967 (1207908)	
Almond Green	—	Nov 1970 (1288024)	Saloon
		Jul 1969 (1257418)[3]	Traveller
Trafalgar Blue	—	Nov 1970 (1288377)	Saloon[4]
	Nov 1967 (1205081)	Jul 1969 (1257371)[3]	Traveller
Maroon 'B'	Oct 1967 (1200480)	Jul 1969 (1257425)[3]	Traveller[5]
Peat Brown	Oct 1967 (1200534)	Nov 1970 (1288376)	Saloon
		Jul 1968 (1227264)	Traveller
Snowberry White	Oct 1967 (1200773)	Nov 1970 (1288281)	Saloons
		Jul 1969 (1257181)[3]	Traveller

Notes

[1]A dash indicates that the colour continued in use from 948cc models.

[2]Except where an additional date is given for Traveller models, the final chassis number listed is for the saloon version, which continued in production until November 1970. The same colours were used for 1098cc convertibles until their discontinuation in June 1969 – the last convertible chassis number was 1254328. Where a different starting/finishing number or date has not been quoted for the Traveller, the introduction or discontinuation of the particular colour occurred on Travellers at the same time as on saloons and convertibles.

[3]These numbers refer to the last of the Cowley-built Travellers. Detailed records giving colours for individual chassis numbers are not available for Adderley Park built Travellers from July 1969.

[4]Chassis number 1288377 was the last saloon.

[5]Chassis number 1257425 was the last Cowley-built Traveller.

OPTIONAL EXTRAS & ACCESSORIES

Relatively few optional extras were available for 1098cc models. On the pre-1964 cars a heater still had to be specified on Standard models, but post-1964 a new 2.8kw heater was fitted as standard and a larger 3.8kw version became available as an optional extra. Whitewall tyres were offered as an export option and Dunlop SP 145-14 radial tyres became available late on in production. Reclining seats were also briefly offered as an extra and are featured in 1970 versions of the driver's handbook – one of the few places they are likely to be seen today!

Seat-belts were available initially as an accessory, supplied and fitted by distributors and dealers. Static belts (front and rear) or 'automatic' inertia reel belts (front only) were available. Following seat belt legislation, static belts were fitted in the front as standard from 1 January 1971, other types having to be specified as an optional extra.

The following accessories were available for 1098cc models:

Wing mirrors
Door-mounted driver's side mirror
Boot-mounted luggage rack
Roof rack (rigid)
Rear fog lamps
Driving lamps (front)
Reversing lamp
Tow bar and towing hitch
Radiator blind
Seat covers
Travelling rugs (various)
Supplementary tool roll
Aluminium wheel discs (set of four)
Rimbellishers
Locking petrol cap
Roof-mounted radio aerial
Chrome exhaust extension piece/finisher
Exhaust deflector
Badge bar (chrome)
Rubber floor mats in red or black, or with Morris 1000 designation for front footwells only
Chrome sill finishers
Wooden gear lever knob with Morris or BL motif
Heated rear window kit (Smiths)

PRODUCTION CHANGES

CHANGES BY CAR NUMBER

990290 (Sep 62)
First 1098cc engine fitted to Minor 1000. New style of air cleaner assembly installed.

1039564 (two-door saloon) (Sep/Oct 63)
1040520 (Traveller)
1043271 (convertible)
2.8kw fresh air heater introduced as a kit. Air intake integrated into radiator cowl. Redesigned windscreen washer system. External key-operated lock fitted to left-hand door.

1043218 (two-door saloon) (Oct 63)
1043226 (Traveller)
1043271 (convertible)
1043752 (four-door saloon)
Zone toughened windscreen introduced. New design of combined side/flasher lamps at front and rear. Windscreen wiper blades lengthened and now work in tandem. Extra round amber light fitted to rear of Traveller.

1060095 (Mar 64)
3.8kw fresh air heater available as an optional extra.

1082280 (two-door saloon) (Oct 64)
1082284 (four-door saloon)
1082537 (Traveller)
1082717 (convertible)
New design of fascia panel. Better trim and more comfortable seating with heat-formed vinyl upholstery, monotone on both Standard and Deluxe models. Black-faced speedometer with additional warning light for oil filter. Glovebox on passenger side fitted with lid. Combined ignition and starter switch. New style fascia switches. Swivel ashtrays under parcel shelf. Light Beige crushable sun visors. Plastic-rimmed interior mirror. Two-spoke safety dished steering wheel. Automatic boot lid support. Fresh air heater operation improved.

1159663 (Sep 66)
Sealed beam headlamps fitted. Fuse in sidelamp circuit introduced.

1168813 (Dec 66)
New type of windscreen finisher.

1196653 (Sep 67)
New type of paper air cleaner element introduced.

1248582 (Mar 69)
Start of new engine number series with 10V-189-E-H (or -L) prefix, or 10V-190-E-H (or -L) if fitted with an alternator.

1254328 (Jun 69)
Final convertible car number.

(Late 69)
Oil filter switch ceased to be fitted. Amber warning lens fitted but not used.

1288299 (four-door saloon) (Nov 70)
1288377 (two-door saloon)
Saloon production discontinued.

1294082 (Apr 71)
Traveller production discontinued.

PRODUCTION FIGURES

	Two-door saloon	Four-door saloon	Convertible	Traveller	Total
1962	?	?	?	?	14297[1]
1963	21120	10228	689	13764	45801
1964	18118	61038	660	17083	41899
1965	18379	7945	492	12153	38969
1966	17428	7980	725	12219	38353
1967	17021	7046	462	12853	37382
1968	14067	4315	346	13,85	32213
1969	13528	5014	170[2]	9567	28279
1970	9969[3]	2950[3]	–	10062	22981
1971	–	–	–	3270	3270
Total	–	–	–	–	303443

Notes
[1] Total production in 1962, including 948cc models, was 57,194.
[2] Convertible production ceased in June 1969.
[3] Saloon production ceased in November 1970.

COLOUR SCHEMES (1098cc MODELS)

1962-64 (all models)

Paint	Trim	Carpets	Hood	Grille	Coachline	Wheels
Black[2]	Tartan Red[1]	Red	Pearl Grey	Old English White	Red	Old English White
Dove Grey	Tartan Red[1]	Red	Pearl Grey	Old English White	Red	Old English White
Smoke Grey[2]	Blue-Grey[1]	Blue	Pearl Grey	Old English White	Blue	Old English White
Almond Green[2]	Porcelain Green[1]	Green	Pearl Grey	Old English White	Porcelain Green	Old English White
Old English White[2]	Tartan Red[1]	Red	Pearl Grey	Old English White	Red	Old English White
Rose Taupe[2]	Tartan Red[1]	Red	Pearl Grey	Old English White	Red	Old English White
Trafalgar Blue	Blue-Grey[1]	Blue	Pearl Grey	Old English White	Pearl Grey	Old English White

1964-67/68[3] (all models)

Paint	Trim	Carpets	Hood	Grille	Coachline	Wheels
Black	Cherokee Red	Red	Pearl Grey	Old English White[5]	Red	Old English White
Dove Grey[4]	Cherokee Red	Red	Pearl Grey	Old English White[5]	Red	Old English White
Smoke Grey	Blue Grey	Blue	Pearl Grey	Old English White[5]	Blue	Old English White
Almond Green	Porcelain Green	Green	Pearl Grey	Old English White[5]	Porcelain Green	Old English White
Old English White	Cherokee Red	Red	Pearl Grey	Old English White[5]	Red	Old English White
Rose Taupe	Cherokee Red	Red	Pearl Grey	Old English White[5]	Red	Old English White
Trafalgar Blue[4]	Blue Grey	Blue	Pearl Grey	Old English White[5]	Pearl Grey	Old English White

From Oct 1967 (all models)[6]

Paint	Trim	Carpets	Hood	Grille	Coachline	Wheels
Black	Cherokee Red	Red	Pearl Grey/Maroon[7]	Snowberry White	Red	Dark Silver
Smoke Grey	Blue-Grey	Blue	Pearl Grey	Snowberry White	Blue	Dark Silver
Almond Green	Porcelain Green	Green	Pearl Grey	Snowberry White	Porcelain Green	Dark Silver
Trafalgar Blue	Blue-Grey	Blue	Pearl Grey	Snowberry White	Pearl Grey	Dark Silver
Maroon 'B'	Cherokee Red	Red	Pearl Grey	Snowberry White	Gold	Dark Silver
Peat Brown	Cherokee Red	Red	Pearl Grey	Snowberry White	Snowberry White	Dark Silver
Snowberry White	Black	Black	Black/Maroon[7]	Snowberry White	Red	Dark Silver

1969-70 (Traveller only)[8]

Paint	Trim	Carpets	Hood	Grille	Coachline	Wheels
Blue Royale	Galleon Blue	Blue	-	Police White	Gold	Dark Silver
Faun Brown	Autumn Leaf	Brown	-	Police White	Gold	Dark Silver
Cumulus Grey	Galleon Blue	Blue	-	Police White	White	Dark Silver
Connaught Green	Autumn Leaf	Brown	-	Police White	Gold	Dark Silver
Glacier White	Black	Black	-	Police White	Black	Dark Silver
Bermuda Blue	Black	Black	-	Police White	White	Dark Silver
White	Cherokee Red	Red	-	Police White	Gold	Dark Silver
White	Blue-Grey	Blue	-	Police White	Gold	Dark Silver
White	Porcelain Green	Almond Green	-	Police White	Gold	Dark Silver
White	Black	Black	-	Police White	Gold	Dark Silver

From Jun 1970 (Traveller only)[9]

Paint	Trim	Carpets	Hood	Grille	Coachline	Wheels
Aqua	Navy	Navy	-	Glacier White	Prune	Light Silver
Limeflower	Navy	Navy	-	Glacier White	Prune	Light Silver
Glacier White	Navy/Red/Geranium	Navy/Red	-	Glacier White	Flame Red	Light Silver
Bedouin	Autumn Leaf	Autumn Leaf	-	Glacier White	Blaze	Light Silver
Teal Blue	Limeflower	Olive	-	Glacier White	Limeflower	Light Silver
Bermuda Blue	Navy Blue	Navy	-	Glacier White	Prune	Light Silver

Notes

[1] Deluxe models had duo-tone upholstery, Silver Beige being included to contrast with the main colour.
[2] Colours available on Travellers.
[3] There was a gradual change-over from October 1967 to January 1968.
[4] Not available on Travellers.
[5] Old English White was used for the grille until approximately October 1967, then Snowberry White was substituted for all body colours.
[6] Colour schemes in this section apply to convertibles up to June 1969, Travellers up to June 1970 and saloons up to November 1970.
[7] Although official records and sales brochures list Pearl Grey hoods as standard for all vehicles, Black and Maroon were used on late 1098cc convertibles.
[8] In addition to the other listings, this section covers the more unusual combinations specific to Travellers in the 1969-70 model year. Wheels on Travellers with these colour schemes were painted dark silver.
[9] Wheels on these late Travellers were painted light silver. Some late Travellers also departed from the normal practice of having wing piping matching body colour, having 'ash' coloured wing piping which was presumably intended to match the wood.

LIGHT COMMERCIALS & GPO VANS 1953-71

The arrival of the light commercial range of vehicles was somewhat belated because the first production model did not appear until May 1953. Prototype vans had been on trial as early as 1948 with a view to phasing out the ageing Morris Eight Z-type van, but it was the impetus provided by Morris's merger with Austin which brought the project to fruition and got the Light Commercial Vehicles (LCVs) on the road.

Part of the incentive was to meet the needs of the GPO, which was anxious to have a quarter-ton vehicle of proven reliability. The Morris Minor certainly fitted the bill, as subsequent sales proved. For a short time, the Z-type and the new O-type Morris Minor quarter-ton van and pick-up models were assembled side by side at Cowley. Production gathered pace and Minor LCV sales exceeded 48,000 between 1953-56.

Updates to the general range of Morris Minors were incorporated in the vans and pick-ups, and over the years Series III 948cc and Series V 1098cc models were produced. Badge-engineered Austin variants, designated Series C, proved popular after their introduction in early 1968, but the fact that

these are still regarded as Morris Minors is a telling comment on the tradition and history associated with these popular vehicles.

In order to keep costs to a minimum, the GPO insisted on certain unique specifications for its mail vans and engineering vans. BMC obliged, the GPO was happy, and as a result these special contract vehicles remained in demand right to the end of production in 1971, by which time an estimated 50,000 had been supplied. Although these unique vehicles share most of their components with the standard light commercial vehicles, some of their specifications differ markedly.

Sadly, the history of all of these fine (and now rare) light commercial vehicles cannot be fully documented as some of the production records were lost at Adderley Park after the plant closed down. Nevertheless, it is possible to document some of their original features and to appreciate just how versatile they were.

BODY & CHASSIS

Unlike Morris Minor cars, the LCVs retained the use of an all-steel, box-

This extremely rare 1954 Series II pick-up in Platinum Grey was rescued by the author from a scrapyard and restored to original specification. A canvas tilt was an optional extra on pick-ups. Now owned by Martin O'Dowd, this pick-up is still on its original chassis.

From the rear, the separate stop/tail and indicator lamps distinguish this Persian Blue 1971 Austin Series C model, owned by Ian Hawkes, from earlier pick-ups. The design of the optional canvas tilt remained unchanged throughout production.

A delightful and rare 1958 pick-up, painstakingly restored by Neville Wright, finished in Sandy Beige and fitted with the 948cc A-series engine. If a passenger seat was specified as an optional extra, the spare wheel was fixed behind the cab on a special bracket. The pick-up's separate cab back is joined to the cab roof along the line of the sealing rubber.

sectioned, full-length chassis frame. In so doing, an element of continuity was maintained with the pre-war era and the war years. Such was the success of the LCV chassis design that it remained in production virtually unchanged until late 1971, as the last version of the Morris Minor to be made.

The cab was built in unit construction with the bulkhead, inner flitch panels, scuttle, windscreen inner and outer surrounds, door B posts, sills, inner floor and roof panel to form the basic vehicle. A separate cab back which bolted to this main structure was fitted for pick-up models, quoted as an option for purchasers ordering a chassis/cab, and omitted on vans. Rearwards of the cab, an all-steel van back or pick-up back could be specified as a factory option. The customer's other choice was to take delivery of a chassis/cab and fit a custom-designed back to it.

The van back comprised two side panels, a roof panel and two rear doors. Internally, two inner wheelarch panels were enclosed by metal inner side-to-floor panels and the space in between – the main floor area – was made up of two wooden floor panels. Cross rails were fitted front and rear: the front one supported the wooden floor and the front edge of the side panels, while the rear one supported the rear sections and housed the number plate panel and rear-mounted rubber buffers.

A similar arrangement applied to the pick-up. Two side panels and a hinged tailgate provided the outer structure. The internal structure of inner wheelarches, side-to-floor panels, wooden floor and cross rails was identical to the van's. The tops of the side panels were designed so that four metal hoops could be secured in order to provide a framework for an optional canvas tilt.

Other body parts specific to the commercial vehicles included the bonnet and the front bumper blades. The bonnet is distinctive in that there is no provision for side-mounted badges or side finishers, thereby making the doors – which are

This rare 1954 Series II GPO telephone engineer's van has been returned to its original specification by Peter Hanby, its current owner. The distinctive rubber wings were shared with contemporary mail vans. An opening windscreen, which provided additional ventilation for the driver, and associated roof-mounted windscreen wipers are other distinctive features on all early split-screen GPO vehicles.

Owned by David Preston, this 1969 Royal Mail van, complete with period advertising on the side panel, did its rounds in Winchcombe, Gloucestershire.

interchangeable with a four-door saloon's front doors – appear incongruous because they incorporate the normal moulding for a coachline. The front bumpers, always painted silver, are equally distinctive and give the impression that they are too short, indicating the cost-saving measures employed to make the LCVs competitively priced.

The other parts of the body – wings, doors, front bumper valance and grille panel – were interchangeable with similar series car models in the range, and were updated as and when new specifications were introduced. One significant change unique to the commercials was the introduction of larger

windows in the van's rear doors from the start of Series V production in September 1962.

The GPO vehicles shared the same chassis as standard LCVs, but special towing and lifting brackets were fitted to the rear corners of the chassis.

On the first of the GPO mail and engineers' vans, the main body differed in several respects, the most notable being the use of rubber front wings. Although they are viewed as something of a novelty today, these unique body parts were fitted both to absorb low-speed impacts and to save money. A further significant difference confined to

these early split-screen vans was an opening front screen on the driver's side. This provided additional ventilation, a useful facility due to the fact that a heater was not fitted and the screen had a tendency to mist up. This opening screen also meant that, contrary to normal practice, the wipers had to be mounted on the cab roof.

The rubber 'bumpers' fitted to the rear of the Series II and Series III GPO vans had a bevelled profile instead of the normal rectangular shape, but Series V models reverted to a more conventional appearance by using rectangular rubbers. A further difference unique to all the GPO vehicles

Seen here in appropriate surroundings, this 1972 telephone engineer's van owned by Roland Turner displays the final yellow livery used by the Post Office – and a memorable advertising slogan of the time.

Many of the unique features of the Series II quarter-ton commercial vehicles are shown here: a painted centre screen pillar, a plain windscreen rubber without a bright insert, black wiper arms and a black mirror, the latter being a standard fitting which was screwed and tapped into the windscreen pillar.

was the addition of an inspection trap in the rear wooden floor. This detachable wooden cover was secured by a budget lock and key, provision being made for storage of the key by the addition of a sprung metal clamp.

BODY TRIM

Brightwork on the Series II LCVs was restricted to the bonnet flash, bonnet hinges, bonnet badge, hub caps, door handles and escutcheons, door striker plates, hockey sticks and top grille bar.

Unlike Series II cars, there was no provision for a chrome insert in the windscreen rubber and the centre windscreen pillar was painted body colour. The previously chromed bumper blade was painted silver and the wiper arms were painted black. Door window frames were painted body colour and the quarterlights

on early vehicles were fixed, although a conversion kit later became available to allow opening quarterlights to be substituted.

An additional feature on early vehicles was the use of an exterior mirror on the driver's side windscreen pillar; the body of the mirror and the arm were painted black. This arrangement was initially carried forward to the Series III, but at van number 69624 mirrors were fitted to the wings. A further change in the use of mirrors occurred on Series V and Series C vehicles when sprung mounting brackets were incorporated into the wing-mounted versions.

A number of specialised items of equipment, largely concerned with security, were specified by the GPO and fitted to mail and engineers' vans.

The rear doors were of standard construction, but those on mail vans had

This Series III pick-up differs substantially from the Series II. Note the stainless steel windscreen wipers, bright insert in the windscreen rubber, and single-pane windscreen. Unlike car models, the bonnets of all light commercials lack waistline mouldings and side badges, and the door window frames are painted body colour. Mirrors are now mounted on the wings, out of shot here.

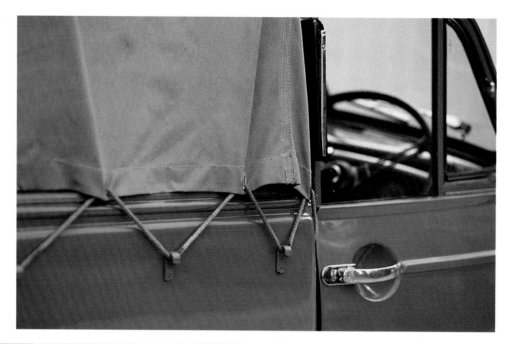

A pick-up fitted with the optional canvas tilt would have brackets screwed to the side panels in order to tie down the canvas sides. Light commercials use the same 'short' doors and door handles as the four-door saloons.

Apart from having a shortened and painted front bumper blade, the nose treatment differs little from car models. This wing is to original specification: note the smooth profile of its inner edge adjacent to the headlamp.

wire mesh security grilles on the inside of the rear windows and an additional exterior steel locking bar – activated by a pull mechanism which the driver could operate from his seat – to supplement the normal lock. A half-sized, wooden-framed wire mesh grille was fixed to the van body immediately behind the driver's seat on mail vans, this feature being enlarged on telephone engineers' vans into a full-width partition which effectively separated the cab from the van back. It was common practice for the spare wheel to be mounted on this panel. Instead of a steel locking bar on the rear doors, engineers' vans used a hasp and padlock in addition to the normal lock.

All of these GPO features continued in use throughout production, but an additional security improvement was introduced for Series III models when Yale locks were fitted

to both driver and passenger doors in 1957. Located just below the quarterlight and forward of the main window glass, the lock was linked to the door handle mechanism by a metal rod to allow the exterior handle to remain inoperative with the door closed. Only when the key was placed in the lock and turned did the rod mechanism engage and allow the door to be opened. Credit for this ingenious, if somewhat unconventional, system rests with Reg Job, who was one of the original Morris Minor design team.

LIGHTING

Standard lighting arrangements continued in use except for the wing-mounted Lucas headlamps used on rubber-winged GPO versions and the absence of indicators or trafficators on Series II LCVs.

An aluminium 'crinkle' grille and an Austin badge on a slightly modified bonnet were unique features of Austin-badged Series C versions.

The rubber wings and proud headlamps fitted to Series II GPO vehicles seem incongruous today. Original replacement wings are scarce.

Additional security on Royal Mail vans included mesh grilles for the rear windows, a locking bar, and provision for a padlock to be fitted (below).

Royal Mail vans left the factory in their full livery, which extended to the roundel on the door (above). The additional Yale lock represented a determination to improve security.

Large Winfield wing mirrors were fitted to late model Royal Mail vans.

A wooden ladder (right, above) was stowed on a steel rack on the roof of the telephone engineer's van until 1969, when lighter replacements in aluminium (right, below) were introduced.

Special externally-fitted Lucas trafficators were available as an extra on Series II light commercials.

Although the headlamps on rubber-winged GPO vans were similar in general style to those fitted to early Morris Eight Z-type vans, they were larger and featured a broad chrome bezel on the leading edge of the exposed black headlamp bowl.

A further unique feature of the GPO mail and engineers' vans was the use of special flashing indicators. Roof-mounted indicators, unflatteringly dubbed 'pig's ears', were fitted as standard on the last 168 split-screen models, continued on Series III models and were only phased out when separate rear indicator lamps were fitted in addition to the stop/tail lamps on 1098cc models. At this point the flat rear lamp lenses were also replaced by the domed ones used on Traveller models.

Owing to the lack of indicators or trafficators on Series II LCVs, some enterprising owners fitted 'pig's ears' or an alternative solution of specially-designed, externally-mounted trafficators. The latter, mounted high on the B posts, had a fixing arrangement which managed to overcome the problem of the extra vehicle width presented by the curvature of the van back.

INTERIOR TRIM

The interior trim on the commercial vehicles was at best adequate and at worst spartan. Comfort certainly left something to be desired on early vans and pick-ups, especially where a heater was not part of the original specification.

Functional one-piece black rubber floor mats were used on all models throughout production, and covered the inner floor area to leave the inner sills and wheelarches exposed in the painted body colour. Owing to changes in the profile of the gearbox covers fitted to the different series of vehicles, several different mats were produced.

Headlinings on the early Series II versions were three-piece Rexine-covered boards. These continued in use for a time on Series III models before being replaced by a one-piece cloth headlining. Initially this cloth headlining was light grey, but pale grey was introduced for the 6cwt and 8cwt Austin and Morris models.

Interior trim panels were plain. Door panels on Series II and Series III models were

brown, while on the Series V they became Arizona Beige at first and black in the final years of production. These colours were always matched on the seats fitted to the respective models. The design of Series II seats closely matched those used in contemporary saloons, Travellers and convertibles both in pattern and in the style of seat frame, but thereafter the seat patterns were unique to the Series III, Series V and Series C vehicles and totally different from anything else in the Morris Minor range.

As on car models, the Series II seat frame initially used an interlocking spring arrangement for the seat base support. The driver's seat had a hinged backrest, and the pattern on the covers on both backrest and base was five vertical narrow fluted panels flanked by two broader panels. This pattern was carried forward when a second type of Series II seat frame with a solid base was pressed into service. The passenger seat – which had to be specified as an optional extra – had the facility to be tipped and folded.

The later Series III/V/C style of seating used similar seat frames to other models in the Morris Minor range, but the three broad

The optional canvas tilt is supported by four steel hoops. The body colour inner wheelarch panel, black inner side panel and painted wooden floorboards are to original specification. Since this pick-up has no passenger seat, the spare wheel is carried in the cab.

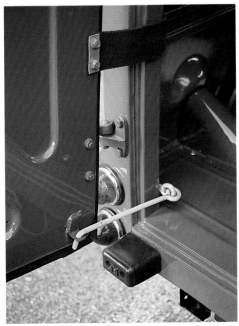

The change from a single stop/tail lamp on early models (above) to separate stop/tail and indicator lamps on Series V and Series C models (right) required redesigned side panels on both van and pick-up versions.

trim panels on the base and backrest provided a distinctive workmanlike appearance and in service proved to be durable and hard-wearing. Although three different colours were used during the period 1956-71, there was no significant change in style. As on the Series II, the passenger seat was an optional extra, the previous tipping and folding arrangement continuing.

Two types of colour-matched door pull were featured. On the first type, used on the majority of LCVs, the pull was fastened directly to the door frame, the aperture in the trim panel having a finisher to prevent excessive wear. The second type, rarely used on commercials, followed the conventional Minor arrangement whereby the pull was fastened through the trim and secured to the inner door frame.

A further detail difference from Minor cars relates to the front edge of the parcel tray. On early models this was a metal strip which was usually painted brown, but midway through Series III production a crash pad was substituted. In the majority of Series III vehicles this crash pad was brown, but vehicles finished in primer had black crash pads. All Series V and Series C models also had black crash pads.

Some interior fittings differed on the GPO vehicles. On very early models the seats followed the plain black pattern of the previous Z type and were mounted on special sliders for easier adjustment. These seats were phased out quite quickly in favour of the later LCV variant of Series II seats, but the trim on GPO vehicles was always

The van's 78 cubic feet of load space in the rear – along with a further 12 cubic feet beside the driver if a passenger seat was not fitted – proved a strong selling point. Note the location of the spare wheel on a van when a passenger seat is installed.

A half-sized wood-framed wire mesh partition was a feature of the Royal Mail vans (below). Although none of these vehicles ever had a passenger seat when in service, one has been fitted here so that the owner doesn't always have to travel alone!

The pick-up's hinged tailgate(above), supported on each side by a chain within a vinyl leathercloth sleeve, provides easy access to the spacious loading bay. If a passenger seat is fitted, the spare wheel is mounted on the cab back on the passenger side. The inner side panels, painted black on Series II vehicles, were painted body colour on subsequent models, as seen here.

The telephone engineer's van (this is a Series II version, left) was fitted with a variety of specialised equipment. The wood-framed wire mesh partition had several purposes: as well as acting as a safety barrier and providing a mounting point for the spare wheel, it served as the front support for a stepladder. The sleeved chain hanging from the roof is the rear support for the stepladder. Pruning forks were stored at floor level and placed on the aperture beneath the spare wheel.

The storage bins dominating the load space of this late telephone engineer's van are similar in style to those of earlier versions, but they are now made of aluminium.

black instead of brown. In subsequent series of GPO vans, seat patterns always closely resembled those used in civilian LCVs, although black was the main GPO colour.

Door trim panels on GPO vans differed, comprising metal panels secured by cross-headed screws. Chrome-plated door pulls, each secured by four cross-headed screws, were fitted because the doors were subjected to frequent use on these public service vehicles. Floor coverings at first followed the normal LCV style of a one-piece moulded rubber mat, but when it became clear that these were insufficiently durable a more substantial block type rubber covering was introduced for GPO models after van numbers 85256 (Mail) and 85902 (Engineers'). Roof linings followed the Series II style of three-piece board lining until the end of Series III production, at which point a one-piece fabric lining with wire tensioners was introduced.

DASHBOARD & INSTRUMENTS

The basic nature of the commercial vehicles left them bereft of some of the creature comforts and finishing touches associated with their saloon, convertible and Traveller counterparts. Apart from the need to specify a heater and passenger seat as options, the absence of indicators or trafficators on Series II LCVs was a notable shortcoming which led some owners to fit either of the two systems described in the 'Lighting' section. As a consequence, many early vehicles have

A painted wooden dashboard panel is rarely seen, although this was standard on early light commercials. The pouch on the passenger side is a first aid kit. The Bakelite dashboard-mounted trafficator switch is original, but the extra white lever below it has been added by the owner in order to operate additional flashing indicators.

This partially restored cab shows clearly the brown seats fitted to Series II light commercials. The steering column and the front edge of the parcel shelf are correctly painted gold, while the gearbox cover panel is black. Glovebox liners have yet to be fitted to this vehicle, and non-standard carpet covers the wheelarch panels and inner sills.

Black trim was used on later Series V models, and this 1971 model – which the steering wheel horn push identifies as an Austin version – has a steering lock. Other features worthy of note include the black rubber floor covering and the position of the courtesy light switch.

Plain brown door panels with matching button fasteners and door pulls are the correct features for Series II light commercials. The door sealing rubber also has a brown fabric covering. The trafficator switch, if fitted, is the same as that used on two-door saloon and convertible models.

extra owner-added dashboard switches, but in due course Series III vehicles acquired the same indicator arrangements and steering column stalk as the rest of the range.

The only other significant difference on regular LCVs was the absence of glovebox lids on all vehicles except the earliest Series IIs, built before February 1955. Home and export versions of these early vehicles had a full-width wooden dashboard as standard, but 'civilian' customers could specify the option of a metal cover panel for the small speedometer mounted in front of the driver, a corresponding metal glovebox lid incorporating the Morris motif on the other side of the dashboard, and an additional central grille panel.

The dashboard layout on the GPO mail and engineers' vans mirrored that of other LCVs of the same series, except that early

Series II vehicles were always fitted with the standard LCV specification wooden dash panel which shrouded the separate speedometer, fuel and oil gauges Another minor GPO difference is that Series III models fitted with the earlier 803cc engine, gearbox and 5.375:1 rear axle had a different speedometer.

All other dashboard and instrument features on LCV and GPO models were the same as those used on other production Minors.

ENGINE

The same A-series engines were fitted to the standard production commercials as to the rest of the range: 803cc to Series II, 948cc to Series III and 1098cc to the 6cwt/8cwt Austin/Morris variants. As a rule, low

A wicker mail storage basket occupied the passenger seat space on a Royal Mail van.

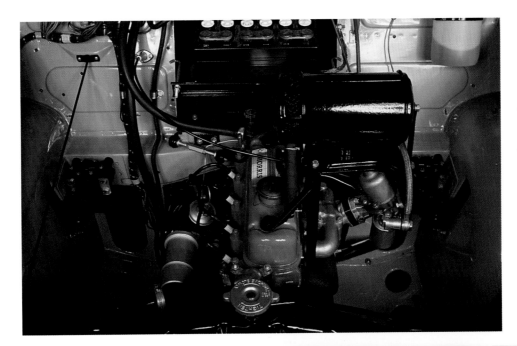

This engine bay, with its 803cc A-series unit correctly painted light blue instead of the far more common green, shows some features peculiar to light commercials, such as the shock absorbers being painted black and the battery tray in black instead of body colour. Small departures from originality include the use of jubilee clips (instead of wire ones) and the addition of a period accessory windscreen washer.

compression engines were fitted as standard and high compression engines were an option. The type of engine fitted would be evident from the identification code preceding the engine number, as follows: 803cc, APHM; 948cc, 9M-U-L (except early APJM); 1098cc, 10MA-U-L (until 1969) or 10V-189-E-L (from 1969).

As on the cars, green was the dominant colour for Morris engines throughout LCV production, although light blue was a rare exception on some Series II vehicles. Austin variants, however, differed significantly in that the engine block and rocker cover were black. The Austin label on the rocker cover matched its Morris counterpart in being black on silver.

Of all the differences between civilian LCVs and GPO models, the most surprising is the choice of engines. In what can only be assumed to have been a cost-saving exercise, the 803cc overhead valve engine continued in use on mail and telephone engineering vans until 1964, as was also the case on contemporary disabled persons' versions of the Minor 1000. This gave rise to the odd situation, therefore, where no 948cc-engined GPO vehicles went into service.

The 1098cc engine and all the associated standard mechanical components were used between 1964 and 71.

The situation with the Morris 803cc engines in GPO vehicles is further complicated by variations in the engine type used. The following identification codes and explanatory notes summarise the position:

Engines on the Austin versions were painted black, but otherwise all components and ancillaries are shared by Austin and Morris models. Shock absorber arms should correctly be painted black on all light commercials.

Engine	Use	Notes
8M	GPO	Standard engine
8MA	GPO	Hybrid crankcase
8MC	GPO	Lucar connections

The 1098cc engines also had some variations applicable to the GPO vehicles and export versions. The full range of Morris 1098cc engine types is as follows:

Engine	Use	Notes
10MA	Civilian LCVs	Standard issue
10MC	GPO	Fitted with governor
10ME	Export	Positive crankcase ventilation
10MJ	Colonial[1]	Standard unit
10ML	Colonial[1]	Positive crankcase ventilation

[1]This terminology is believed to indicate use for CKD kits assembled abroad.

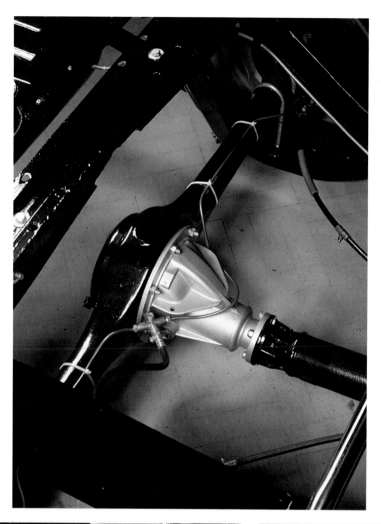

The basic rear axle layout, seen here on a Series II, was similar to that of car models, but 1098cc light commercials used a different ratio.

The mounting for the side-exit exhaust and the rear spring locating points differ significantly on commercial vehicles.

The 4½J wheels fitted to late commercials are much sought-after by enthusiasts. UK regulations required the exhaust to exit from the offside.

FUEL SYSTEM

The LCVs used the same SU type L fuel pump and the same range of SU carburettors fitted to corresponding car versions, the only major fuel system difference relating to the petrol tank. An altered filler position meant that the angle of the filler pipe was significantly different from that on the saloon, Traveller and convertible models. The use of the 5-gallon tank was greatly extended on commercial vehicles, the capacity being increased to 6 gallons for later versions only.

EXHAUST SYSTEM

The exhaust system used on commercial vehicles differs from that on all other models in that it exits from the body at the side instead of the rear, but the mounting arrangements at the manifold parallel the type used on similar series cars and the familiar floor-mounted asbestos heat shield remained in use. In order to comply with UK regulations, the exhaust had to exit from the offside on home market models, so the piping consequently runs across the chassis behind the cab.

Chassis-mounted support brackets secure the exhaust in position. Home market models were originally fitted with a four-piece exhaust system, but left-hand drive models used a shorter three-piece system which exited from the body on the opposite side to right-hand drive versions.

ELECTRICS

With the exception of the amendments necessary to the wiring loom to take account of variations in the lighting arrangements for the commercial vehicles, the main electrical components are identical to those described for each of the series of cars.

TRANSMISSION

Among the transmission and rear axle components, the only change for the LCVs was to the differential. The Series II vehicles used a semi-floating rear axle and had a ratio of 5.375:1. Later Series III models and the 6cwt/8cwt versions with a three-quarter floating rear axle all used the 4.55:1 differential, which represented a departure from standard practice for 1098cc models as the cars used the taller 4.22:1 ratio. As with the rest of the range, all components were painted black.

SUSPENSION

The basic principles of the Morris Minor suspension apply to the LCVs, differences being confined to variations in the components.

Armstrong telescopic shock absorbers were used at the rear of all LCVs in place of the standard lever arms. The number of leaves in the rear springs varied during production. Seven leaves were used on early Series II models, but this number was increased to eight from van number 6043. No further change occurred until the 8cwt versions were introduced late in production, at which point the thickness of the leaves was increased and their number reduced to seven.

Corresponding amendments occurred on the front suspension with the introduction of the 8cwt Austin and Morris versions, which had strengthened suspension uprights, steering levers and torsion bars. A modification to the front suspension occurred on GPO vehicles in 1959, when

The substantial box section chassis is evident on this Series II van, as are robust light commercial features like the beefy type of Armstrong telescopic rear shock absorber and the eight-leaf spring. The shape of the bump stop rubber is also different on commercials. The plastic ties securing the copper brake pipe (less durable steel pipes would have been used originally) are a temporary measure while the correct metal ties are located.

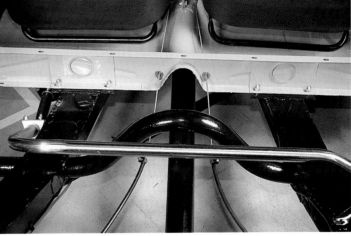

This view of the rear cab mounting panel shows the arrangement for the longer handbrake cables used on commercial vehicles.

jacking brackets were added to the front lower suspension arms; earlier models were updated retrospectively.

STEERING

All LCVs use rack and pinion steering. Modifications introduced on cars were replicated on each subsequent series of commercial vehicles, except that the stronger steering levers used on 6cwt and 8cwt variants are unique to these models. These components are not interchangeable with earlier versions or with those fitted to cars.

Black wheels were part of the specification for GPO vehicles. The recommended tyre pressure is marked on top of the wheelarch in white on the telephone engineer's van (right) and in black on the mail van (below). The use of 'town and country' tyres was a GPO option often taken up for mail vans used for rounds in rural areas.

BRAKES

With three exceptions, the braking system and all its components remained unchanged for the light commercial vehicles. First, a longer flexible brake hose was used at the rear at the union adjacent to the rear axle. Second, modified handbrake cables gained an aluminium sleeve to take account of the need for them to be mounted on the chassis and for them to pass through the base panel of the cab back. Third, a modification peculiar to some GPO vehicles (generally those used in rural areas) was the addition of mud deflectors to the brake drums.

WHEELS & TYRES

Variations in the wheels and tyres used on the regular vans and pick-ups were confined to the later models, as the 803cc and 948cc versions used the same 4J wheels and Dunlop 5.00-14 tyres as the cars. The 1098cc LCVs were supplied with Dunlop 5.20-14 tyres, while the introduction of the 8cwt vehicles resulted in larger wheels and tyres being

fitted, the rims increasing in width to 4½J and the tyres to 5.60-14.

Wheels on Series II vans and pick-ups matched the body colour, Series III variants had aluminium-coloured wheels, and later 6cwt and 8cwt models had dark silver wheels in keeping with the rest of the range. Chromed hub caps with the M motif were used until plain hub caps were substituted just before the introduction of the Austin 6cwt and 8cwt vans. Recommended tyre pressures differed from car models. On most vans and pick-ups the recommended figures were 24lb/sq in (front) and 28lb/sq in (rear), increasing to 27lb/sq in (front) and 30lb/sq in (rear) on 8cwt models.

On pick-ups the spare wheel could be stored inside or outside the cab. It was bolted to the outside back of the cab if a passenger seat was fitted, or to the inside of the cab back on the passenger side (to give more load space) if a passenger seat had not been specified. In the case of the van, it was recommended that the spare wheel be bolted to the inside of the body on the passenger side opposite the tool roll, which

was secured to the body pillar behind the driver's seat.

Wheels on GPO vehicles were the same type as those fitted to civilian vans and pick-ups, but differed in being painted black. Hub caps were dispensed with after 1962 as part of continuing cost-cutting efforts. An interesting GPO feature was the display of the recommended tyre pressures at the edge of each wheelarch. On the majority of models the lettering was white, but during the final years of production this was changed to black on mail vans and mid bronze green on the new yellow livery introduced for telephone engineering vans in 1968. An exception to the normal lettering position applied on the rubber wings fitted to early models. In this case, the lettering appeared on the narrow metal strip fitted on the back edge of the front wings.

TOOL KIT

The tool kit supplied with the Series II LCV vehicles was fairly comprehensive. Unlike the jack supplied with the cars, the LCVs had a screw jack which the workshop manual described as a triple-lift type. Instructions for its use were precise in the driver's handbook: 'When raising a rear wheel, the jack should be placed below the seventh (early models) or eighth (late models) spring leaf as close to the axle as possible. When raising a front wheel, the jack should be located below the front suspension arm approximately 8½in (216mm) from the centre line of the torsion bar'!

Up to van number 108755, the tool bag contained the following items: screw jack with lifting handle, tyre lever, tommy bar, grease gun, tyre pump, plug spanner, screwdriver, tyre valve spanner, axle drain plug key, distributor spanner and gauge. These early commercials had a separate starting handle and combined wheel brace and hub cap remover.

After van number 108755, the tool kit was considerably depleted and owners were encouraged to purchase a supplementary tool kit from their distributor. The later tool roll contained only the following items: screw jack with lifting handle, tyre lever, tommy bar, wheelbrace and hub cap remover. A supplementary tool kit similar to that described earlier for 1098cc saloons was also available and recommended for owners of commercial vehicles.

The tool kit supplied with GPO vehicles differed in many respects. On Series II and

The identification plates on Series II light commercials are the same as those used on other Morris Minors. This wiring loom, rebraided to the original appearance complete with red tracers, is the correct type for all Series II cars and commercials.

Series III vehicles, the tool roll was distinguished from that of other LCVs in that it had ties instead of a buckle fastening. In addition to the normal items, the tool kit included a foot-operated tyre pump, sprung metal clip for stowage of the starting handle, sump plug box spanner and wooden-handled Philips screwdriver. Unusually, a starting handle guide complete with fixing screws was also part of the tool kit. In keeping with civilian LCVs, the GPO tool kit was considerably reduced for later series vehicles.

IDENTIFICATION, DATING & PRODUCTION

All Series II LCVs and some early Series IIIs had the same type of chassis and patent plates attached to the bulkhead as on the cars. The codes used operated as follows with three letters and two figures, although the second figure was omitted on later models:

First letter Indicates model of vehicle, always **O** for quarter-ton van on Series IIs.

Door-mounted identification plates were fitted to late Series V and Series C models. Whereas the regular light commercials have standard door panels and door pulls (above left), the GPO versions were unique in having metal door panels, metal door pulls and security-inspired shortened quarterlight catches (above right).

PRODUCTION FIGURES
LIGHT COMMERCIAL VEHICLES

Year	Van	Pick-up	Chassis/Cab	Total
1953	3374	838	60	4272
1954	10992	3591	460	15043
1955	?	?	?	18381
1956	?	?	?	13860
1957	?	?	?	16167
1958	?	?	?	15369
1959	?	?	?	15990
1960	13676	3290	211	17177
1961	16614	3819	164	20597
1962	11682	3057	133	14872
1963	12073	2463	20	14566
1964	12506	2596	23	15125
1965	14222	2342	12	16576
1966	11406	2048	8	13462
1967	13652	3288	36	16976
1968	22572	2959	–	25531
1969	20839	3974	–	24813
1970	17210	3083	–	20293
1971	24137	3439	–	27576
Total				**326627**

Note
Figures for the different models are not available for the period 1955-59.

Second letter Indicates type of vehicle: **E**, van; **F**, pick-up; **G**, cab chassis; **H**, GPO mailvan; **I**, GPO engineering van; **K**, plain chassis.

Third letter Indicates the colour: **B**, Light Grey; **C**, Dark Red (on GPO mail vans); **D**, Dark Blue; **E**, Green; **F**, Beige; **H**, Primer or CKD Finish.

First figure Indicates class of vehicle: **1**, RHD home; **2**, RHD export; **3**, LHD; **4**, North America; **5**, CKD RHD; **6**, CKD LHD.

Second figure Indicates type of paint finish: **1**, Synthetic; **5**, Primed.

Later Series III models from 1962 onwards follow the changed practice adopted for cars in 1958 and described earlier. The first prefix letter denotes the make of the vehicle – M for Morris. The second letter indicates the engine type – A for A-series. The third letter is for the body type – such as V for van or U for pick-up. The fourth letter gives the series of the model, and the fifth letter is an optional prefix used when the vehicle differed from standard RHD, such as L for LHD.

A third type of identification plate was used on later 6cwt and 8cwt models and fixed to the inside of the passenger door. As well as recording the vehicle identification code and chassis number, it also included details about weights. These later vehicles also had an additional plate attached to the bulkhead indicating the BS conformity of the seat belt anchorage points.

Although the codings for the LCVs are relatively straightforward, the sheer number of variants means that it can be difficult to keep track. The accompanying table is a simplified identification profile for the main home market models and includes details of the first and last known car numbers for each series. As production records are not available for the later vehicles, the last official chassis number is quoted for all Series V and Series C vehicles – although the author knows of some unofficial claims of surviving vehicles with higher chassis numbers.

The following list of chassis numbers, when used in conjunction with the 'Production Changes' section, provides a useful guide to dating a light commercial vehicle.

Series II 803cc LCV

1953 (May)	501
1954 (Jan)	5215
1955 (Jan)	21360
1956 (Jan)	38781
1956 (Sep)	49767

Series III 948cc LCV

1956 (Sep)	49801
1957 (Jan)	52066

1958 (Jan)	68229
1959 (Jan)	84282
1960 (Jan)	100242
1961 (Jan)	118556
1962 (Jan)	137653
1962 (Sep)	149536[1]

Series V 1098cc LCV[2]

1962 (Sep)	149537
1963 (Jan)	153629
1964 (Jan)	168224
1965 (Jan)	183447
1966 (Jan)	202221
1967 (Jan)	213680
1968 (Jan)	235634[3]
1969 (Jan)	258624
1970 (Jan)	281896
1971 (Jan)	302806
1971 (Dec)	327369[4]

Notes

[1] 149536 is the last official Series III chassis number listed in factory publications. However, in 1962 production of light commercial vehicles was split between plants at Abingdon, Cowley and Adderley Park. Some doubt exists over the precise cut-off point for 948cc production, and there is evidence to suggest that some 1098cc light commercial vehicles had chassis numbers lower than 149536. In addition, some confusion exists over the designation of Series III to light commercial vehicles. While factory publications clearly designate 948cc models as Series III and 1098cc models as Series V (Austin being Series C), contemporary sales brochures carried the Series III designation forward to early 1098cc models.

[2] Factory records do not exist for Series V commercial vehicles beyond 1964, so the chassis numbers quoted here for the period 1965-71 have been taken from Glass's Commercial Vehicle Check Book.

[3] Austin 6cwt Series C vehicles were introduced in 1968 at chassis 236504, and Austin 8cwt versions started production at chassis 238597.

[4] 327369 is generally accepted as the chassis number of the last commercial vehicle to be produced – a GPO van.

OPTIONAL EXTRAS & ACCESSORIES

Optional extras on the standard commercial vehicles included a radio, a heater, a canvas tilt and a passenger seat for vans. An addition to the usual range of accessories for each series of vehicles was a tonneau cover for pick-up models.

LIGHT COMMERCIAL VEHICLE IDENTIFICATION

Model	First	Last
Morris Quarter-ton Van (Series II)	OE-501	OE-49767
Morris Quarter-ton Van (Series III)	OE-49801	OE-149536
Morris 6cwt Van (Series V)	M-AV5-149537	M-AV5-327369
Morris Quarter-ton Pick-Up (Series II)	OF-501	OF-49767
Morris Quarter-ton Pick-Up (Series III)	OF-49801	OF-149536
Morris 6cwt Pick-up (Series V)	M-AU5-149537	M-AU5-327369
Morris Quarter-ton Chassis and Cab (Series II)	OG-501	OG-49767
Morris Quarter-ton Chassis and Cab (Series III)	OG-49801	OG-149536
Morris 6cwt Chassis and Cab (Series V)	M-AQ5-149537	M-AQ5-327369
Morris Quarter-ton GPO Postal Van (Series II)	OHC-3554	OHC-67196
Morris Quarter-ton GPO Postal Van (Series III)	OHC-67197	OHC-164615
Morris 6cwt GPO Postal Van (early Series V)	OHC-177641	OHC-216200★
Morris 6cwt GPO Postal Van (late Series V)	M-AG5-223801	M-AG5-327369
Morris Quarter-ton GPO Engineering Van (Series II)	OJE-2999	OJE-68000
Morris Quarter-ton GPO Engineering Van (Series III)	OJE-85137	OJE-174398
Morris 6cwt GPO Engineering Van (early Series V)	OJE-176001	OJE-216550★
Morris 6cwt GPO Engineering Van (Late Series V)	M-AE5-225801	M-AE5-317045
Austin 6cwt Van (Series C)	A-AVC-236504	A-AVC-327369
Austin 6cwt Pick-Up (Series C)	A-AUC-236504	A-AUC-327369
Austin 6cwt Chassis and Cab (Series C)	A-AQC-236504	A-AQC-327369
Morris 8cwt Van	M-AV5-238597	M-AV5-327369
Morris 8 cwt Pick-Up	M-AU5 238597	M-AU5-327369
Morris 8cwt Chassis and Cab	M-AQ5-238597	M-AQ5-327369
Austin 8cwt Van	A-AVC-238597	A-AVC-327369
Austin 8cwt Pick-Up	A-AUC-238597	A-AUC-327369
Austin 8cwt Chassis and Cab	A-AQC-238597	A-AQC-327369

★Estimated figure

COLOUR SCHEMES

1953-56 (quarter-ton 803cc Series II)

Body colour	Seats	Floor mats	Headlining	Grille	Wheels	Dates
Platinum Grey	Brown	Black	Beige	Platinum Grey	Platinum Grey	To Feb 55
Dark Green	Brown	Black	Beige	Dark Green	Dark Green	To Feb 55
Azure Blue	Brown	Black	Beige	Azure Blue	Azure Blue	Throughout
Beige	Brown	Black	Beige	Beige	Beige	To Feb 55
Sandy Beige	Brown	Black	Beige	Sandy Beige	Sandy Beige	From Feb 55
Clarendon Grey	Brown	Black	Beige	Clarendon Grey	Clarendon Grey	From Feb 55
Empire Green	Brown	Black	Beige	Empire Green	Empire Green	From Feb 55
Primer	Brown	Black	Beige	Primer	Primer	Throughout

1956-68 (quarter-ton 948cc Series III and 6cwt 1098cc Series V)

Body	Seats	Headlining	Grille	Wheels	Van interior	
Sandy Beige	Brown	Light Grey	Sandy Beige	Aluminium	Stone	To May 58
Empire Green	Brown	Light Grey	Empire Green	Aluminium	Stone	To May 58
Blue	Brown	Light Grey	Blue	Aluminium	Stone	To May 58
Clarendon Grey	Brown	Light Grey	Clarendon Grey	Aluminium	Stone	To Feb 59
Dark Green	Brown	Light Grey	Dark Green	Aluminium	Stone	May 58 to Feb 59
Connaught Green	Brown	Light Grey	Connaught Green[1]	Aluminium	Stone	Feb 59 to Oct 61
Frilford Grey	Brown	Light Grey	Frilford Grey	Aluminium	Stone	Feb 59 to Jul 60
Birch Grey	Brown	Light Grey	Birch Grey	Aluminium	Stone	May 58 to Jul 60
Yukon Grey	Brown	Light Grey	Yukon Grey[1]	Aluminium	Stone	Jul 60 to Oct 61
Pearl Grey	Brown	Light Grey	Pearl Grey[1]	Aluminium	Stone	Jul 60 to Oct 61
Rose Taupe	Brown	Light Grey	Old English White	Aluminium	Stone	From Oct 61
Almond Green	Brown	Light Grey	Old English White	Aluminium	Stone	From Oct 61
Dove Grey	Brown	Light Grey	Dove Grey	Aluminium	Stone	From Oct 61
Old English White	Brown	Light Grey	Old English White	Aluminium	Stone	Believed from 65
Primer	Brown	Light Grey	Dove Grey	Aluminium	Stone	Throughout

1968-71 (1098cc Austin Series C and Morris Series V)

Body colour	Seats	Headlining	Austin grille	Morris grille	Wheels	Van interior
Snowberry White	Arizona Beige	Light Grey	Dark Silver Grey	Snowberry White	Dark Silver	Snowberry White
Everglade Green	Arizona Beige	Light Grey	Dark Silver Grey	Snowberry White	Dark Silver	Everglade Green
Primer	Arizona Beige / Black	Light Grey / Pale Grey	Dark Silver Grey	Snowberry White	Dark Silver	Primer
Peony Red	Arizona Beige	Light Grey	Dark Silver Grey	Snowberry White	Dark Silver	Peony Red
Cumulus Grey	Arizona Beige / Black	Light Grey / Pale Grey	Dark Silver Grey	Snowberry White / Glacier White	Dark Silver	Cumulus Grey
Damask Red	Arizona Beige / Black	Light Grey / Pale Grey	Dark Silver Grey	Snowberry White / Glacier White	Dark Silver	Damask Red
Persian Blue	Arizona Beige / Black	Light Grey / Pale Grey	Dark Silver Grey	Snowberry White / Glacier White	Dark Silver	Persian Blue
Glacier White	Black	Pale Grey	Dark Silver Grey	Glacier White	Dark Silver	Glacier White
Connaught Green	Black	Pale Grey	Dark Silver Grey	Glacier White	Dark Silver	Connaught Green

Note

[1] Old English White became the grille colour from 1960.

PRODUCTION CHANGES (LCV)

SERIES II

501 (May 53)
First light commercial vehicle produced, with 803cc engine and designated Series II.

2185 (Sep 53)
Fixed glass in quarterlight discontinued, conversion kit available for fitting opening glass retrospectively.

2287 (Sep 53)
Accelerator cable abutment bracket modified.

4951 (Dec 53)
Hub assembly modified.

5459 (Jan 54)
Seats modified: fluted trim pattern retained, but solid seat base replaces previous interlocking spring design.

6043 (Jan 54)
Number of leaves in rear springs increased from seven to eight.

21563 (Jan 55)
Black piping discontinued on front wings.

22330 (Feb 55)
New dashboard with open gloveboxes replaces former wooden dashboard with optional metal lids and central grille. Revised frontal styling: new grille panel and grille with horizontal bars, redesigned front valance and 'hockey sticks', and wings incorporating sidelamps.

34936 (Oct 55)
Hub bearing nut on left-hand side of axle changed to left-hand thread.

45842 (Apr 56)
Change to battery clamp bar and fixing: new shape bar with sealing rubber and revised fitting position. Circular rubber blanking cover in battery tray discontinued, rectangular plastic sealing pad introduced.

46289 (May 56)
New style of gearbox cover, providing more space for foot pedals.

49767 (Sep 56)
Last Series II LCV.

SERIES III

49801 (Sep 56)
First Series III LCV. Features include single-pane windscreen, 948cc engine, uprated gearbox, revised gearbox cover, 4.55:1 rear axle ratio, new shape rubber floor mat, new style steering wheel, column-mounted indicator stalk, push-button handbrake, revised wipers with motor in engine bay. On pick-ups, number of side panel hooks reduced from 20 to 16.

50037 (Oct 56)
Sun visor colour changes from beige to light grey.

50869 (Nov 56)
Seat frame modified, new brown seat upholstery with broad panels.

54686 (May 57)
Arm assembly for front door checks modified.

55235 (Mar 57)
Windtone horn mounting position changed.

55488 (Mar 57)
Mirror mounted on A-post given revised arm.

57270 (May 57)
Rubber-mounted circular rear reflector replaced by rectangular reflector with chrome bezel on vehicles exported to Switzerland.

57504 (May 57)
Fabric headlining replaces three-piece board type. This is the official change point, but 34 earlier vehicles (between 57293 and 57465) were fitted with a fabric headling.

69624 (Feb 58)
Mirrors now fitted to front wings, with 3½in arms.

86439 (Feb 59)
Fascia tray modified to take account of heater fittings for fresh air vent; glovebox liners modified.

94552 (Sep 59)
Combined horn push and indicator switch discontinued on UK models.

101098 (Jan 60)
Metal clip for door sealing rubber on B-posts introduced.

104980 (Mar 60)
Wing mirror arms increased in length to 4⅞in.

108755 (Jul 60)
Tool kit reduced in size.

136928 (Nov 61)
Export models fitted with DR3A wiper with 100° angle of wipe; UK models followed at chassis 137576.

148734 (Aug 62)
Roof-mounted interior light and courtesy light switches fitted.

149071 (Aug 62)
Column-mounted indicator stalk with green bulb fitted to vans, together with DB10 relay unit. First pick-up with this change was 147889.

149566 (Sep 62)
Last Series III LCV.

SERIES V AND SERIES C

149567 (Sep 62)
First Series V model with 1098cc engine, and uprated gearbox in line with car models; larger 7¼in Borg & Beck dry plate clutch, 4.55:1 rear axle ratio retained. Larger 8in front brake drums fitted in conjunction with new master cylinder. New two-spoke steering wheel. Van rear doors fitted with larger windows and revised sealing rubber. New style Windtone horn with revised mounting bracket. Stainless steel hub caps instead of chrome-plated.

165483 (Oct 63)
Revised wiper arrangement: tandem operation with 120° angle of wipe. Introduction of 2.8kw fresh air heater with 'elephant's trunk' ducting.

165725 (Oct 63)
Revised pressing for fascia panel; different mounting for windscreen washer bottle.

171659 (Mar 64)
Rectangular rear reflector with chrome bezel replaces circular design.

183512 (Jan 65)
New fascia featuring black-faced speedometer, anodized backing panel and revised toggle switches. Black crash pad on fascia tray. New light beige sun visors with 'crushable' safety design, swivel mountings and retaining hooks.

233568 (late 67)
Plain hub caps introduced.

236504 (early 68)
Austin Series C 6cwt models introduced: Austin bonnet badges and horn push, 'crinkle' slatted grille, plain hub caps. Rear springs on 6cwt models (Morris and Austin) now have eight leaves, Arizona Beige door panels and seat covers introduced.

238597 (Apr 68)
New Morris and Austin 8cwt models: changes include wider 4½J wheels, stiffer steering levers, stronger front suspension uprights, modified rear springs with seven thicker leaves. Plain hub caps on both Morris and Austin models.

302806 (Jan 71)
Steering column lock fitted to some models.

327368 (Feb 72)
Last non-GPO Series V LCV.

PRODUCTION CHANGES (GPO)

SERIES II

OJE 2999 (Oct 53)
OHC 3554
First Series II GPO engineers' (OJE) and postal/mail (OHC) vans. Features common to both are 803cc engine, rubber wings, wooden dashboard/fascia, toughened glass for cab windows, laminated rear door windows, 5.375:1 rear axle, eight-leaf rear springs, SN3205/05 speedometer, circular rubber blanking seal on bulkhead in battery tray, internal partition behind driver's seat, chromed iron hub caps.

OJE 3195 (Jan 54)
OHC 3800
Brown seats replaced by GPO specification black seats with fibre seat slides.

OJE 3196 (Jan 54)
Guard pruning hook amended.

OJE 11267 (Jun 54)
OHC 8985
Amendment to steering rack lubrication.

OJE 11785 (plus 19001-19196) (Jan-Feb 55)
OHC 9455 (plus 19280-19444)
Last of rubber wing vehicles. Except for additional batches, steel wings now fitted as standard.

OJE 19015 (Nov 54)
OHC 9379
Engine tie rod added.

OJE 19197 (Nov 54)
OHC 9456
Metal fascia and SN4401/09 speedometer fitted.

OJE 28001 (May 55)
OHC 29201
Coil moved from bulkhead to mounting on dynamo.

OJE 42109 (Mar 56)
OHC 43483
Starting handle guide bracket discontinued.

OJE 42326 (May 56)
OHC 43607
New style of gearbox cover with separate master cylinder cover panel; revised one-piece rubber mat.

OJE 42353 (May 56)
OHC 43619
Radiator top modified to incorporate rubber overflow pipe.

OJE 42686 (Oct 56)
OHC 43853
Last of vehicles with rubber flap fitted to bottom of front wing inner edge.

OJE 42692 (Oct 56)
OHC 43858
Sun visor colour changes from beige to light grey.

OJE 43189 (Jun 57)
OHC 44265
Battery clamp modified and new sealing rubber introduced. Circular bulkhead blanking disc replaced by L-shaped plastic insulator in battery tray.

OHC 44267 (Jul 57)
Budget lock on rear door replaced by Yale lock.

OJE 59371 (Oct 57)
OHC 59027 (Aug 57)
New design of black steering wheel replaces old beige or light grey steering wheels; push-button handbrake introduced.

OJE 59438 (Jan 58)
OHC 67082
Clutch pedal shaft modified.

OJE 59442 (Jan 58)
OHC 67097
Speedometer changed to SN4406/08.

OJE 59449
OHC 67104
Rear left-hand chassis fixing added for fuel pipe.

OJE 59458 (Jan 58)
OHC 67114
Rear axle bump stop rubber modified, new type ACA 8008 road wheels fitted.

OJE 67775 (Oct 58)
OHC 67409
Distance piece fitted to front suspension lower link.

OJE 85136 (Jan 59)
OHC 67196 (Mar 58)
These are designated as the last split-screen vehicles, but OHC 68000 (registered UXH 917) is believed to be the last Series II vehicle with an opening windscreen.

SERIES III

OJE 85137 (Jan 59)
OHC 67197 (Mar 58)
First Series III GPO engineers' (OJE) and postal/mail (OHC) vans. Unlike other light commercials, 803cc engine retained and designated 8MA (first engine number is 1218). Changes include one-piece laminated windscreen, revised bonnet, Yale locks instead of Union locks.

OJE 85902 (Feb 59)
OHC 85256 (Jan 59)
Former one-piece floor covering replaced by link mats with rectangular pattern.

OJE 85250 (Jan 59)
OHC 85320
Glovebox liner modified.

OJE 85893 (Feb 59)
OHC 85371
Battery tray liner modified.

OJE 85973 (Mar 59)
OHC 85500
Door seal surround protectors introduced.

OJE 97661 (Feb 60)
OHC 98119
GPO jacking brackets fitted to front suspension lower arms.

OJE 102806 (Mar 60)
Rear windows and windscreen change from laminated to toughened glass.

OJE 120678 (Aug 61)
OHC 116662 (May 61)
Interior light switch mechanism altered.

OJE 117188 (Jun 61)
OHC 116765
Number of body-to-cab bolts reduced from 16 to 12.

OJE 120783 (Sep 61)
OHC 130601 (Jul 61)
Rear mud flaps introduced and Smiths recirculatory heater fitted as standard.

OHC 130780 (Dec 61)
Additional security plate fitted below quarterlight catch on cab doors.

OJE 138000 (Jan 62)
OHC 138261
Rear door grille panels discontinued, link matting reduced to driver's side only.

OJE 138235 (Jul 62)
OHC 147021
Revised handbrake assembly.

OJE 153137 (Dec 62)
OHC 147161
Rear axle casing changed from ATA 7351 to BTA 610; rear wheel cylinders modified.

OJE 155974 (Feb 63)
OHC 155001
Rear door windows enlarged; revised grilles fitted on mail vans (OHC).

OJE 162096 (Oct 63)
Revised front wings incorporating amber/white indicator/sidelight units. Modified bulkhead assembly with provision for ducting for revised 2.8kw fresh air heater.

SERIES V

OJE 176001 (Aug 64)
OHC 177641
First Series V GPO engineers' (OJE) and postal/mail (OHC) vans. The 1098cc engine introduced (no GPO vehicles had 948cc engine), with 10MC designation. New gearbox in line with car models, revised gearbox cover panel, larger 7¼in Borg & Beck clutch, 4.55:1 rear axle. SN4477/00 speedometer, one-piece fabric roof liner, metal braided fuel pipe from pump to carburettor, ACA 8199 wheels, rectangular rear reflectors. Brown seat trim, but only OJE models have a passenger seat. OJE models also gain the quarterlight security plate fitted to OHC models during Series III production.

OJE 177409 (Jan 65)
OHC 178438
Revised dashboard with anodized backing panel and chrome strips, black-faced speedometer of type SN4419/02. New light beige sun visors with 'crushable' safety design. Key starter switch introduced, but the following chassis numbers were anomalies which continued with a pull starter: OJE 177422/177423/177425/ 177481; OHC 178439/178441/178445/178449/178450/ 178466.

OJE 209019 (1966?)
OHC 208084
Threaded seat belt mounting points introduced.

OHC 214951 (1967?)
Mud flaps fitted front and rear.

Hereafter, precise records of production changes are sketchy, but the following points are worthy of note:
1. Black seat covers returned for GPO models in 1968.
2. Roof ladders and rack in aluminium were introduced for M-AE5 models in 1968.
3. M-AE5 models were painted yellow from 1968.
4. The final chassis number was M-AG5 327369 (a mail van) manufactured in December 1971.

BUYING AND RESTORATION

The main features on the underframe of the monocoque show clearly on this 1962 two-door saloon. Of particular note are the front chassis legs, tie plates and rear spring hanger brackets.

Anyone contemplating full or partial restoration to original specification of a Morris Minor can do so safe in the knowledge that there is an extensive network of specialist restoration and parts firms. In many respects, Minor owners are pampered compared with owners of other classic cars because of the availability of a wide range of off-the-shelf parts, particularly for later Minor 1000 models. For earlier models, however, the situation is not so good and owners often have to be more enterprising in their quest for parts and in their efforts to retain originality.

A useful starting point in determining the originality of any Morris Minor is the factory records, which are held by the British Motor Industry Heritage Trust (BMIHT) at Gaydon in Warwickshire. For a fee, a certificate can be provided listing the build date of the vehicle and detailing its original specification.

BODY

That the Morris Minor has survived in greater numbers than most of its contemporaries is due in no small part to its well-designed monocoque body and to the added protection provided by the roto-dip process which ensured that the shells received adequate anti-corrosion treatment – but the contribution of dealer-added underseal treatments is less certain. All the same, the Minor can suffer badly from rust

This replacement late front wing has been modified to accept the smaller side/indicator lamp unit fitted to 948cc and early 1098cc Morris Minor 1000 models.

problems, and sometimes in areas which are not immediately apparent.

Bodyshell areas most prone to rust include the A posts (especially on the concealed front edges where they butt up to the back of the front wings), the bottom of the B posts, the outer sills (along the perimeter of the floor) and the accompanying box sections (concealed beneath kick plates). Perhaps the single most significant problem area is the central crossmember, whose top surface can be seen by lifting the seats and raising the carpet. If excessive cracking or bubbling is present, a major task can be anticipated in replacing the whole crossmember. On later cars fitted with jacking points it is common to find that these have rotted through.

On the underside, special attention needs

to be paid to the front chassis legs. These should be carefully examined not only for rust but also for signs of metal fatigue, particularly where the front suspension is attached and in other places where these important structural items may have been used as jacking points. Similar checks should be made at the rear spring hanger mounting points, where it is common to find evidence of cracking on the floor.

Attention under the bonnet should focus on the top of the inner wing (particularly where it joins the bulkhead), the tie plates in the bottom of the engine bay, and the panel immediately below the radiator. Examination of the spare wheel compartment should take account of the stresses caused by the rearward spring hanger

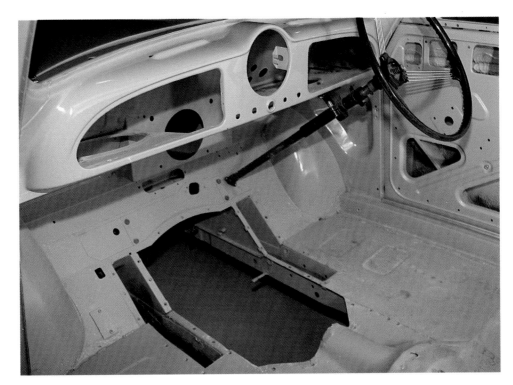

This repainted 1962 passenger compartment provides some useful reference points for would-be restorers. The aperture just below the battery box is the vent for the fresh air supply to the Smiths recirculatory heater, while the openings either side of the gearbox 'tunnel' are the chassis legs. On right-hand drive models the brake master cylinder is located within the offside leg, and vice versa for left-hand drive.

mounting. In the boot area, the top edge of the inner wing, which houses the caged nuts for wing mountings, should be thoroughly checked for signs of weakness.

All external body panels are attacked by rust: wings, doors, boot lids and grille panels all present particular difficulties for the restorer with a keen eye for originality.

Later Minor 1000 front and rear wings are still produced using the original presses. As the different styles of wings fitted to the Series MM, Series II and early Minor 1000 models are not generally available, modifications are often carried out to Minor 1000 wings in order to create the correct profile and ensure that the apertures for light fittings are authentic. In the case of 'high-headlamp' Series MM wings, for instance, the aperture can be eradicated altogether and the obtrusive Minor 1000 joint removed. Even the elusive 'low-headlamp' front wings, which are virtually unobtainable as 'new old stock', can be based on Minor 1000 wings by using the rear sections in conjunction with the remnants of original wings or newly fabricated metal. Rear wings for Series MM and Series II vehicles had a significantly different profile from later Minor 1000 rear wings, but can be re-created by recutting Minor 1000 wings. Such work clearly comes at a price, but these modifications could be carried out by a competent sheet metal worker.

Replacement doors and boot lids are not available. Both tend to rot out on the bottom

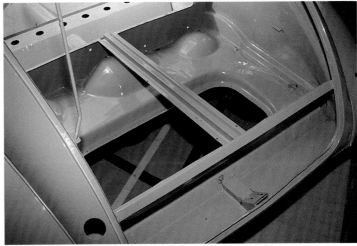

edges and repair panels are available. Doors, however, need to be jigged if a repair panel is used to replace all of the bottom section. Later grille panels are now available new, and if necessary the bottom section – which tends to be the part that corrodes – can be transplanted onto earlier grille panels.

ENGINES

Of the four engines fitted to the Morris Minor, the 918cc sidevalve is the rarest and presents the most parts supply problems, but sufficient parts are available from specialist suppliers to allow units to be reconditioned. Clubs such as the Morris Minor Owners' Club and the Morris Register do source original parts, a process which is helped by

The boot area showing the fuel tank aperture (at bottom left), the centre support rail for the boot floor, and the rear crossmember which runs under the trailing edge of the rear seat. The portions of the rear inner wings which will remain exposed within the boot area when all the fittings are installed have yet to be painted black.

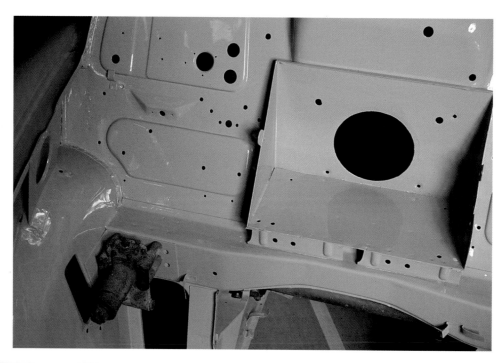

This repainted bulkhead illustrates well the size and position of all the apertures which were part of the original pressing on a 1962 saloon. The large hole in the battery tray is a legacy from the rotadip rust-proofing process.

On early models the windscreen wiper motor was located behind the dashboard panel. A new arrangement, first seen on Minor 1000 models, used this new mounting bracket on the nearside front wheelarch panel.

the fact that many components are shared by the Morris 8 Series E. Another useful source which has recently come to light is the sidevalve unit supplied to the army for use as a starter engine for tanks. Although modification is needed for use in Morris cars, this is proving to be a popular solution.

The A-series engines – 803cc, 948cc and 1098cc – are robust and uncomplicated. Longevity is their trademark and there are few recurring faults. Of the three, the 803cc version – generally regarded as being under-powered – is the weakest and spares for it are becoming scarce, but there is still a reasonable supply of secondhand units. Parts availability for the 948cc and 1098cc engines is good and reconditioned units are readily available. In addition, the option now exists for 'lead-free' cylinder heads to be fitted.

TRANSMISSION

The Series MM gearbox is generally regarded as a thoroughly dependable unit, the most typical problem relating to the gear lever conical spring, which can adversely affect gear changing and which can sometimes break up.

Later gearboxes used in conjunction with the A-series engines have a number of weaknesses which the prospective buyer or restorer would do well to check out. The main problems relate to the absence of synchromesh on first and reverse gears. Excessive wear on the gear teeth resulting from repeated crashing of the gears can lead to problems such as gear whine and a familiar tendency to jump out of gear. Effective repairs can only be carried out following a complete strip down. Alternatively, replacement gearboxes are readily available for 948cc and 1098cc models. An exchange service is offered by some specialist engineering firms and a number of Morris Minor parts suppliers also stock replacement units. The 803cc units present more difficulties as the parts necessary to recondition them are in short supply. Enterprising owners resort to making one good gearbox out of components salvaged from several others, and enlisting the skills of a specialist to complete the rebuild.

With the rear axle, the original advice offered in the workshop manuals urged owners to seek the advice of their Morris dealer if they encountered problems with the rear axle, for a range of special tools is required to make repairs. The final get-out, said the factory, was to "fit a replacement unit". Alas, fitting a new replacement unit or visiting the local Morris dealer are no longer options, but fortunately there are a number of specialist engineering firms who will recondition rear axles.

STEERING

The rack and pinion steering used on all Morris Minors rarely presents any difficulties. Replacement racks are available and it is also possible to have existing units reconditioned.

Early steering wheels can create difficulties when they crack and split as replacements are scarce, and only to be found at auto-jumbles. The plastic finish also has a tendency to soften, the resulting sticky residue sometimes having a devastating effect on upholstery. The black dished steering wheel and later two-spoke safety wheel fitted to Minor 1000 models, however, are still in plentiful supply secondhand.

SUSPENSION

Most suspension components are either available as new units or capable of being reconditioned. One exception relates to early Series MM front suspension swivel pins, which are unique and not interchangeable with the later Minor 1000 type. The critical feature is the size of the stub axle. Both early and late types are the same length, but their diameters are different. On the Series MM the diameter is ⅞in maximum and ⅝in minimum, while on the later 1000 type the respective dimensions are 25mm and 17mm. The favoured solution, which allows original MM hubs and road wheels to be retained, is to have the hub machined out to take 25mm and 17mm inner diameter bearings.

New front suspension legs are no longer available, but refurbishment of original items is possible by means of a specialised metal respray technique which enables the threads to be recut to original specification. Top links and trunnions are still available from Morris Minor parts suppliers. Rear springs are also available new, although retempering services exist for original items. Concours *aficionados* tend to have the leaves powder-coated prior to reassembly. Reconditioned front and rear shock absorbers are readily available.

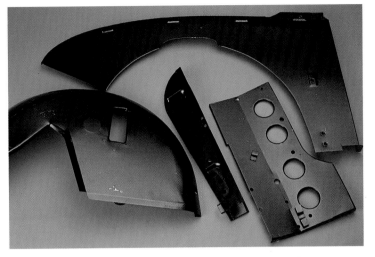

A wide range of remanufactured panels is available for structural repairs. Shown here (clockwise from left) are an inner flitch panel, inner wing panel, A-post panel and tie plate.

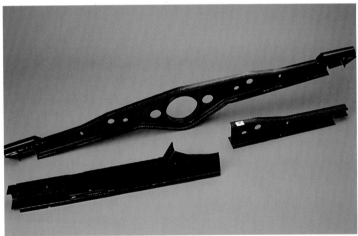

Major chassis repairs often involve the replacement of the central crossmember and the front chassis legs. A complete crossmember, a crossmember end repair section and a half chassis leg are shown here.

Late Series II and 948cc Minor 1000 models share the same rear axle, distinguished by the absence of an oil filler plug on the casing.

INTERIOR TRIM

The whole of the Morris Minor range is well catered for when it comes to replacing interior trim, but restoration to precise original specification is a forlorn hope as many of the original trim materials are no longer available. That said, many of the substitute materials used in trimming kits come very close to matching the originals.

Seat and trim panels for early Series MM cars are the most difficult to return to original specification. The distinctive beige upholstery is difficult to match because of the graining pattern, but also partly as a result of the variation in colour brought about by ageing. The problems also occurs, but to a lesser extent, with the choice of patterns for Series II trim. The Minor 1000 models, however, benefit from much-improved

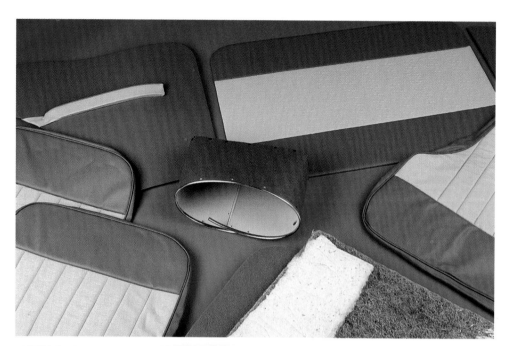

Full kits for the replacement of interior trim are available for most models. This kit is for a duo-tone interior in blue-grey and silver beige. Included are front and rear seat covers, door and rear side panels, a glovebox liner and front seat padding.

The ash on Traveller models is structural and subject to MoT regulations. A full service for the supply, fitting and maintenance of Traveller wood is available from specialist companies.

replica materials, particularly for duo-tone upholstery and the later heat-formed trim.

The four-piece board headlining fitted in the Series MM and early Series II models can pose problems. The very early felt-type cloth covering can be replicated, but the later Rexine covering is unobtainable and so care has to be taken to mix and match from secondhand materials if a lot of repair is needed. The same applies to Series II Travellers, which retained the board head-lining throughout production. Replace-ment headlinings are available for later Minor 1000 models, although once again they are not an exact match. Having said that, they come very close, they are manufactured to a very high standard, and they come complete with fitting instruc-tions. Regrettably, Series II owners who have vehicles with the early dark beige fabric headlining will be disappointed as a suitable

replacement has not yet been found.

A similar situation exists with carpet, as the original Karvel is no longer available. Replacement carpet sets are marketed for Minor 1000 models, but some are poor substitutes in terms of colour and quality. Care needs to be taken when ordering new carpet as the gear lever position changed with each of the major updates – and in the case of the Series II during the production run itself. The rubber floor mats fitted to commercial vehicles, Travellers and special order vehicles (such as those supplied to the armed forces) are no longer available and to date no suitable alternative has been commercially produced.

WOODWORK

A full range of solid ash sections is available in assembled or unassembled form from a number of suppliers, the best of whom offer a complete service which includes the supply of specially-commissioned individual sections and complete ash frames for Traveller models, as well as the restoration of sound existing wood.

Problems with Traveller woodwork become self-evident if it is neglected. Discolouration, soft spots and widening joints are all tell-tale signs of deterioration. What isn't always immediately apparent is that the wood is not decorative – it is structural and its solidity should be checked as part of the MoT inspection. The major problem facing the home restorer is whether to take on the task of replacing the wood or

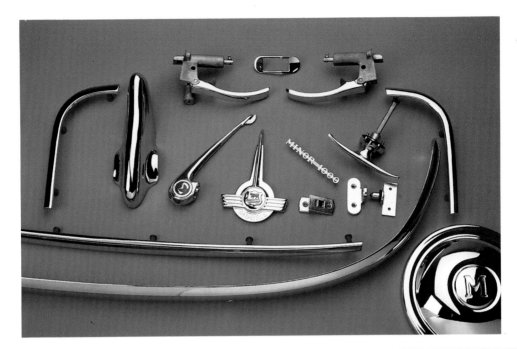

A rare collection of genuine original BMC chromed components. Remanufactured Minor 1000 chromed parts are readily available. The door handles shown here are the type fitted to two-door saloons, convertibles and Travellers.

to enlist the assistance of a specialist restorer. Certainly it is not a project for the faint-heated and three important factors should be borne in mind in making this decision: the need for some relevant DIY experience, the availability of plenty of space in which to work, and having the time to complete the job. The process of replacing Traveller wood has been documented in a number of publications.

BRIGHTWORK

The availability of replacement chromework is generally very good, with components such as bumpers, bonnet and boot hinges, bonnet badges and motifs, exterior and interior door handles, door catches, striker plates, hub caps and hockey sticks all readily found at Morris Minor parts specialists. Improvements to the original specification have been instigated on some remanufactured components. For example, the chrome centre pillar for split windscreen models is chromed brass and the later Minor 1000 rear light unit outer bezel is chromed steel.

At the time of writing, the major brightwork difficulty relates to the early Series MM door top and hinged quarterlight, which were chromed for a time. The availability of sound original items is extremely limited in the UK because the number of home-based cars was small to start with, so solutions include sourcing from abroad or compromising, perhaps temporarily, with later stainless steel assemblies as fitted to Travellers.

Another specific problem at the time of writing is the special badging on the Minor Million limited edition models, but ingenious owners have used two Minor 1000 badges cut and joined in the appropriate place to read Minor 1000000. This practice can be applied to both the large boot badge and the smaller badges on either side of the bonnet. Other rare items include the 'cheesegrater grille' which was fitted as an insert, the early boot handle with an external screw fitting, and the variety of chromed hinges used on sun visors.

LIGHTING

Some of the original light units are becoming increasingly difficult to find as replacement items, particularly the headlamps fitted to 'low-headlamp' Series MMs and, to an increasing extent, the later

Electrical components as fitted to late 1962 Minor 1000 models include (clockwise from the bottom) a Lucas M35G starter motor, Lucas C39 PV-2 dynamo, Lucas LA12 coil, SU type L fuel pump, Lucas 25D4 distributor and Lucas DR3A wiper motor.

These light units are the type fitted to all 948cc and early 1098cc models: a pre-focus headlamp, combined front indicator/side light, rear stop/tail lamp and number plate lamp.

The Lucas DB10 relay unit and flasher unit which enabled flashing indicators to be used with the existing rear lamp unit on late 948cc and early 1098cc models.

A full range of replacement wiring looms is available for all Morris Minor models. The original red tracers, absent from this loom, and many other earlier replacement looms can now be specified.

7in pre-focus headlamps. Sealed beam units have often been fitted instead, so returning to originality means searching at autojumbles and perhaps using services of a resilvering specialist. For understandable reasons, mostly to do with safety, many cars originally fitted with trafficators have had these supplemented or replaced by non-original flashing indicators, a practice which incidentally precluded the use of many fine vehicles, original in all other respects, for photography during the preparation of this book!

Rear light units can also be difficult to source. The single rear light with the centre screw fitted to the first cars is no longer available, and the pedestal mounting used on export models is proving elusive. Fortunately the 'helmet' lamps fitted to later Series MMs and early Series IIs were used by other marques, such as MG, so they are more widely available, even if inflated prices have

to be paid. The lamps fitted to later Series II and 948cc models are in short supply as new units, although the bezels can be rechromed, the bases repainted and damaged lamp lenses replaced with better secondhand ones. New 'old stock' replacements for the distinctive combined indicator/stop light fitted to the 1098cc models are a diminishing commodity, highly priced and much sought-after, but the remanufactured alternative serves the same purpose and to all outward appearances is no different.

Earlier separate pilot lights, later sidelight units, combined sidelight/indicator lamps and Traveller rear lights are available new.

TOURERS & CONVERTIBLES

Tourers and convertibles present a range of quite specific restoration considerations.

First and foremost is the critical factor that the monocoque structure, minus roof, requires considerable bracing prior to any major work – such as replacing the central crossmember, inner floor sections or outer sills – being carried out. Failure to do this will allow the body to flex and cause major problems with panel alignment. Ultimately, the standard of workmanship will be reflected in 'door shutability', the crucial indicator of a convertible's inherent strength and the accuracy of alignment during restoration.

A useful ploy during restoration is to examine carefully a body alignment chart and then set up additional cross-bracing within the parameters of the dimensions offered, by fitting a frame either side of the car on top of the inner sills and attaching it to the inner B post. This can be done in such a way as to allow the doors to remain *in situ* while work progresses. Alternatively, the doors, once adjusted to the correct gap, can be temporarily 'welded' in place with the aid of a couple of strategically placed brackets.

A major problem to have arisen in recent years is the phenomenon of 'converted saloons' or 'chop tops', increasing demand for an ever-dwindling supply of tourer and convertible models having provided the right climate for conversion kits to be marketed to enable owners to transform existing two-door saloons. It is essential that extra strengthening to the original pattern – in the inner sills, at the base of the B post and at either end of the fascia where it joins the A post – is present if structural rigidity is to be maintained. Provided that this work has been done and the rest of the vehicle is intrinsically sound, then there is basically nothing to be concerned about – except that some converted saloons are being passed off as genuine convertibles.

Telltale signs of the 'chop' include uneven welds at the top of the windscreen (although genuine convertible windscreen tops are sometimes transplanted), welded fascia support brackets instead of neatly spot-welded ones, and welded B post support brackets which exhibit signs of uneven welding instead of clean lines. It is worth checking the area concealed by the rear seat squab to investigate whether a roof has been cut off – uneven finishes to leading edges should again sound warning bells. Finally, the inner box sections should always be checked to ensure that extra strengthening has been fitted.

Although there have been instances

The original shape of the top edge of the windscreen surround, as seen here, merits close scrutiny as it is useful to distinguish on an original convertible from a converted saloon.

Fitting correct number plates enhances any restoration. These pressed aluminium plates are authentic for pre-1967 saloons and convertibles.

where chassis numbers have been tampered with and log books amended, it is still worth checking the identification codes on chassis plates. Two-door saloons (MA2S) are quite distinct from convertibles (MAT) on post-1958 cars, while prior to this the presence of the letter C in the prefix denotes a tourer/convertible model – but no distinction was made on the earliest models with the SMM prefix. If there's any doubt, the archive department at the Heritage Motor Centre can confirm the original specification of the vehicle on receipt of chassis number and prefix details.

Other restoration considerations specific to tourers and convertibles relate to the hood and hood frame. On early tourers a replacement celluloid rear window needs to be sufficiently thin to allow it to fold when the hood is down, but the thickness should be increased for the detachable sidescreens otherwise distortion and splitting will result. Hood frames are fairly robust, so new oversized rivets at the pivots are usually sufficient to take up any slack that has developed. All parts are readily available, but it is advisable to enlist the help of a trimming

specialist. It is even more helpful if you have an original pattern to work to if you choose to use the services of a small local trimmer.

COMMERCIALS

Restoration of commercial vehicles to original specification is perhaps the most daunting of undertakings where Morris Minors are concerned. This is borne out by the fact that many owners compromise on originality in order to keep their vehicles on the road. Pick-ups are a case in point: alternative custom-built rear backs are commonplace, while vehicles with the original side panels, inner wheelarch panels and tailgate are few and far between.

Part of the difficulty rests with the un-availability of body panels. Occasionally original stock or good secondhand items come to light at autojumbles. However, some authentic repair panels are available, such as the rear outer wheelarch section on the van or the bottom of the cab back fitted to pick-ups. Replacement panels are also available for the rear inner floor sides and the inner wheelarch panels, but these are not to

Unoriginal Morris Minor? Light commercials remain popular workhorses and useful mobile advertising hoardings, even if some of the services on offer were unimagined in the Minor's day!

original specification. The cab floor and inner sills are available, as is a complete chassis. The chassis accommodates all the datum points of the original design but is improved by the addition of an inner strengthening 'web'.

Items of brown or Arizona Beige trim are difficult to replace to original specification, but black is readily available. Replacement moulded rubber mats are not available, so the easiest solution is to fit black carpets.

GPO mail and engineers' vehicles present even more severe problems because their unique features – such as rubber wings and trim items – are only available secondhand, but occasionally stocks of GPO spares are unearthed. The respective owners' clubs – Morris Minor Owners' Club and Post Office Vehicle Club – are useful contacts for potential leads in sourcing parts.

CONCLUSION

If originality is an overriding concern in the restoration of any Morris Minor, then the foregoing discussion should provide food for thought. If one single area should be singled out as more important than any other, then it has to be interior trim. Such is the variety of trim used in the various series of Minors that a golden rule should be to make its condition and originality high on your priorities. Many owners will vouch for the need not to overlook the detailed and painstaking refurbishment of the trim.

An old saying, patience is a virtue, is particularly apt in the context of classic car restoration. The sourcing of rare original parts can take years, so diligent restorations tend to take a great deal longer than originally anticipated.

CLUBS

The world's largest club is the highly regarded Morris Minor Owners' Club, based in the UK and with a membership of 14,000. For a very modest annual subscription, members can take advantage of cheaper insurance and travel, technical advice, discounted spares and a full calendar of events organised by an extremely active network of 60 branches. The bi-monthly *Minor Matters* is a 36-page magazine with supplements for junior members and classified advertisements.

Other excellent clubs exist throughout the world. Contact addresses are as follows:

UK
Morris Minor Owners Club
Jane White
Membership Secretary
127-129 Green Lane
Derby DE1 1RZ
UK

IRELAND
Irish Morris Minor Club
Noel Williams
3 Turnapin Cottages
Cloghran
Dublin 17
Eire

DENMARK
Nordisk Morris Minor Klub
Box 28
DK-5200 ODENSE
Denmark

SWITZERLAND
Swiss Morris Minor Club
Beat Strickler
Altwiesenstrasse 143
CH - 8051 - Zurich
Switzerland

HOLLAND
Anton Visser
Middelstekamplaan 7
8042 HG Zwolle
Holland

USA
Morris Minor Registry
Tony Burgess
6147 Cheryl Drive
Concord
OH 44077 2416
USA

NEW ZEALAND
Morris Minor Car Club New Zealand
Alan Hoverd
68 Liardet Street
Mornington
Wellington 2
New Zealand

SOUTH AFRICA
Morris Minor Club of South Africa
Gary Dodds
P.O. Box 2127
Jukskei Park
Randburg 2153
South Africa

AUSTRALIA
Morris Minor Car Club of Victoria
Dr David Warren
31 Olive Street
Caulfield 3162
Victoria
Australia

Wollongong Morris Minor Car Club
41 Williamson Street
Corrimal
NSW 2518
Australia